Grounded in firsthand knowledge of an insurgent campaign, *Run Zohran Run!* charts the unexpected rise of Zohran Mamdani and his victory in New York City's 2025 Mayoral Democratic primary.

Mamdani's straightforward platform—a rent freeze, free buses, universal childcare, and city-run grocery stores—cut through the noise of mainstream politics and resonated with working-class voters struggling in an increasingly unaffordable city.

A 33 year-old immigrant who openly identifies as a democratic socialist, Mamdani drew in Muslim and South Asian voters historically sidelined in city politics. His robust support for Palestinian rights upended traditional politics in New York City, where even the most liberal elected officials refuse to criticize Israel.

The campaign faced relentless institutional resistance—attacks from the *New York Times*, the *New York Post*, and vitriol from disgraced former governor Andrew Cuomo and former mayor Michael Bloomberg—but it also demonstrated how Left campaigns can be won.

Whether plunging into the icy water of Coney Island on New Year's Day to promote a rent freeze or letting a Knicks' fan spin a multi-colored basketball on his head at an NBA game, Mamdani's innovative and theatrical campaign captured the public. At the same time, a massive ground operation led by the Democratic Socialists of America mobilized tens of thousands of volunteers to knock on more than 1.5 million doors.

As fast-paced and compelling as its subject, *Run Zohran Run!* reveals how a charismatic candidate and a vibrant grassroots campaign ended a New York dynasty and set the stage for the city's first democratic socialist mayor.

RUN ZOHRAN RUN!

RUN ZOHRAN RUN!

INSIDE ZOHRAN MAMDANI'S SENSATIONAL CAMPAIGN TO BECOME NEW YORK CITY'S FIRST DEMOCRATIC SOCIALIST MAYOR

THEODORE HAMM

OR Books
New York • London

© 2025 Theodore Hamm

Published by OR Books, New York and London

Visit our website at www.orbooks.com

All rights information: rights@orbooks.com

All rights reserved. No part of this book may be reproduced or transmitted in any form or by any means, electronic or mechanical, including photocopy, recording, or any information storage retrieval system, without permission in writing from the publisher, except brief passages for review purposes.

First printing 2025

The manufacturer's authorised representative in the EU for product safety is Authorised Rep Compliance Ltd, 71 Lower Baggot Street, Dublin D02 P593 Ireland (www.arccompliance.com)

Typeset by Lapiz Digital, India. Printed by BookMobile, USA, and CPI, UK.

paperback ISBN 978-1-68219-446-1 • ebook ISBN 978-1-68219-451-5

For Toni, Ellis, and the next New York City

Acknowledgements

Many thanks to Zohran Mamdani and members of his primary campaign team, particularly Andrew Epstein, for their insights and cooperation. Along with numerous longtime friends, so many New York City journalists shared observations with me that I cannot list them all here—because any roster would invariably leave out a few people. Thanks heartily to one and all.

My comrades Liza Featherstone, Ari Paul, John Tarleton, and Ross Barkan were immensely helpful. Urwah Ahmad, my former journalism undergraduate student at St. Joseph's University (NY), provided lots of excellent research assistance. Urwah worked with Zohran at Chhaya, an economic empowerment organization in Queens.

Colin Robinson and his crackerjack team at OR Books—led by Olivia Heffernan—deftly handled the production process (special thanks to Sam Russek for editing). Colin and his crew get credit for the book's snappy title. I will take the blame for any words that irk you.

–T.H.

Contents

Intro: The City Turned Upside Down

Part One: Origins
    1. Cold War, R.I.P. — 17
    2. Roots — 35
    3. Roti and Roses — 49
    4. The Message is a Mantra — 61

Part Two: Ascent
    5. Fast Start — 81
    6. A Spicy Mix — 95
    7. Dodge Charger — 107
    8. Sticks and Stones — 123
    9. A Creative Class — 135
    10. Buckle Up — 147
    11. It's Getting Hot — 159
    12. Five-Alarm Fire! — 171

Part Three: Triumph
    13. The Spoils of Victory — 189

INTRODUCTION
The City Turned Upside Down

On June 25, 2025, just after 12:15 a.m., a victorious Zohran Mamdani stepped on stage at a brewpub in Long Island City, Queens. A 33-year-old Muslim immigrant from Uganda, and an unapologetic democratic socialist, Mamdani had electrified New York City for the past several weeks.

Six months earlier, in mid-January, the Manhattan-based crypto-currency website Polymarket had given the newcomer an 8% shot at winning the mayoral Democratic primary, and although he had not yet become an official candidate, the disgraced former governor Andrew Cuomo—with 100% name recognition—led the pack at 44%. But by election day, Polymarket listed Mamdani at 55%, nine points ahead of Cuomo, who had remained the frontrunner since joining the race in March. The Wall Street crowd knows the trendlines.

Run Zohran Run!

In a hotel room near the brewpub, Zohran scrambled to update his remarks along with campaign manager Elle Bisgaard-Church, political director Julian Gerson, media strategist Morris Katz, and top aide Spencer Goldberg. Coming into the night, they knew that the results had spiked in their favor—but still expected the outcome to be determined after future rounds of ranked-choice ballot tabulations.

The insurgent candidate planned to give a talk along the lines of what a basketball coach tells the locker room after winning the quarter-finals—i.e. "great job everyone, but we're not there yet." But less than 90 minutes after the polls closed at 9 p.m., Cuomo conceded. As they adjusted the speech, Mamdani thought of his youth, when he'd lived in South Africa. He had a quote that he liked.

In his victory speech, which was broadcast live on local TV and across social media, Zohran invoked his native continent's favorite son (and fellow socialist): "Tonight," the candidate calmly began, "we made history. In the words of Nelson Mandela, 'It always seems impossible until it is done.' My friends, we have done it. I will be your Democratic nominee for the mayor of New York City."

Local TV reporters told their mostly older viewers that the upset win was "stunning" and "historic." At election-night watch parties across the city hosted by the Democratic Socialists of America (DSA), of which Mamdani has long been a member, Zohran's army of millennial volunteers went wild. Across the five boroughs—from Ozone Park, Queens, to Kensington, Brooklyn, to Westchester Square in the Bronx—South Asian and Muslim voters of all ages celebrated. Sundry social media platforms lit up.

From the city elite came wails of bewilderment and exasperation. "Terror. Fear. Panic," is how Kathryn Wilde, a ubiquitous spokesperson for the city's dubiously labeled "business community," summed up the collective reaction. As one of the city's largest landlords told the *New York Times*, "You want to have leadership that speaks to what New York is. It's the capital of capitalism."[1] So concurred the extreme-right *New York Post*, which had conducted a smear campaign against Mamdani throughout the primary. On election day, its front page had denounced the insurgent candidate as a "radical, antisemitic socialist." Its follow-up cover page was desperate: "NYC SOS," shrieked the influential tabloid. "Who will save our city after radical socialist batters Cuomo in Dem mayoral primary?" Throughout the city's corridors of power, Mamdani Derangement Syndrome reverberated.

Zohran's quote from Mandela provided his answer to the *Post*'s question. For democratic socialists, it is "we"—not a "she" or "he"—that wins elected offices. When early voting began on Saturday, June 14, Mamdani's massive ranks of volunteers, which surpassed 50,000 by primary day, provided an outreach operation far more genuinely committed to its candidate than that of any mayoral contender in New York City history.[2] A massive number

---

1 For a rundown of similarly hysterical reactions, see *Hell Gate*'s "Morning Spew: Billionaire Meltdown Compilation" (6-26-2025).
2 From the mid-nineteenth century through 1960, Tammany Hall had large election-day operations, and the powerful Democratic Party

of Muslim and South Asian voters, including many in the city's Bangladeshi enclaves, mobilized for the first time in a city election. Although union-friendly, Mamdani received support from only a few local labor leaders,[3] most of whom preferred not to upset the status quo. Zohran's coalition—voters under 50, multiracial, polyglot, pro-Palestine, unafraid to be called socialists—was nothing if not groundbreaking in New York City.

Alexandria Ocasio-Cortez and a diverse array of other local leaders joined Mamdani for a rally on Saturday night, June 14. The candidate and fellow speakers addressed an overflow crowd of mostly twenty-somethings at Terminal 5, a performance venue on Midtown Manhattan's west side. Exponentially more viewers caught clips on social media. "This victory," Zohran declared, "will be historic, not just for who I am—a Muslim immigrant and a proud democratic socialist—but for what we will do: make this city affordable for everyone."

*

Although he did not talk much about Uganda on the primary campaign trail, Zohran never tried to conceal

---

machines in Brooklyn and the Bronx followed suit through the 1990s. Labor unions historically have sent numerous members to help various campaigns. By contrast, Mamdani's volunteers joined based on their own personal motivations.

3   The membership of Local 9 of the UAW is relatively small when compared to other city unions, but it represents many graduate students and thus was quite active in the Mamdani campaign. On primary day, UAW president Shawn Fain issued a rousing video statement of support for Zohran.

his roots among the South Asian diaspora in Africa. On the weekend before the primary, he told an older Black audience at Reverend Al Sharpton's National Action Network headquarters in Harlem that his middle name was Kwame, in honor of Kwame Nkrumah, Ghana's first president and the father of African nationalism. Zohran's mother, acclaimed film director Mira Nair (b. 1957), joined him on the campaign trail, while his father, internationally renowned Columbia University professor Mahmood Mamdani (b. 1946), kept a low profile.[4]

Mahmood Mamdani is a leading scholar of decolonization. As Zohran told the Sharpton gathering, the elder Mamdani risked deportation when he first came to the U.S. by joining SNCC protests in Montgomery. With Spike Lee smiling at The Rev's side, the DSA candidate quoted a Sharpton observation from 2004. It was about the Democrats' long-standing pattern of relying on minority and working-class voters but not delivering anything meaningful in return.

Zohran's nearly 470,000 first-place votes in the primary made him, by vote count, the most popular U.S. politician who fully supports Palestinian rights.[5] On June 25, City University of New York (CUNY) journalism professor Peter Beinart connected Mamdani's success to shifts among younger Jewish voters regarding Palestine. He explained that "social movements often become part of mainstream

---

4   Mahmood Mamdani accompanied Mira Nair at the primary night party.
5   While Bernie Sanders supports Palestinian human rights, he typically criticizes the Netanyahu regime—and does not mention political equality for Palestine.

politics." Until Zohran's successful primary run, the former *New Republic* editor noted, no leading New York City politician had taken a stand on behalf of Palestinian rights. Although "he was very progressive on many issues," Mayor Bill de Blasio (in office from 2014-2021) "made a clear exception regarding Palestine," stated Beinart.[6] Zohran has frequently referred to this stance as progressive except Palestine (or "PeP"). As the CUNY professor observed, even though campus protests in New York City were forcefully shut down by university brass and Mayor Eric Adams' NYPD, Mamdani was now bringing the activists' viewpoint into the electoral realm.

In the homestretch of the primary campaign, State Senator John Liu (b. 1967)—the first citywide Asian-American elected official, who competed against de Blasio for mayor as a left-wing populist in 2013—made a high-profile endorsement of Mamdani and served as one of the speakers at the AOC rally. Attorney General Tish James (b. 1958) similarly lent her influential backing, comparing the attacks on Zohran to the smears Barack Obama had once endured. Alas, the PeP label applies to both Liu and James.[7]

---

[6] The evening after Beinart distributed his comments, de Blasio appeared on *Inside City Hall*, an influential nightly TV program hosted by Errol Louis. To his credit, the former mayor stressed that "disagreements with Israel do not make Mamdani 'antisemitic.'"

[7] Amid the mass famine crisis in Gaza, in late July 2025 Liu and Tish James joined Brad Lander and several other New York elected officials in a statement demanding that Israel allow humanitarian aid into Gaza while calling for an immediate diplomatic resolution of the conflict.

The festive crowd at Mamdani's victory party included a roster of notable Cuomo foes, including James and third-place mayoral finisher Brad Lander (b. 1969), along with countless next-generation leaders.

Mingling within the crowd were anti-monopoly figureheads Lina Khan (like Zohran, a practicing Muslim) and Zephyr Teachout, who challenged then-Gov. Cuomo from the left in the 2014 primary. Actress Cynthia Nixon, who stepped to the plate against Cuomo four years later, continued to express robust support for Zohran.[8] Jamaal Bowman, the DSA Congressman ousted with the help of pro-Israel hawks, caught up with Rep. Nydia Velázquez. Actor and activist Kal Penn, a longtime Zohran pal (who starred in Mira Nair's 2006 film *The Namesake*), gave lots of hugs. Nair and her son's wife Rama Duwaji shed tears of joy. Antigun activist David Hogg, who had cut viral clips with Mamdani as primary day neared, was also in the mix, along with South Asian DSA organizers Jaslin Kaur and Ashik Siddique, respectively representing Queens and Brooklyn.

Two of Zohran's closest DSA allies in the state legislature, Jabari Brisport and Marcela Mitaynes, celebrated with city councilman Chi Ossé, a social media phenom and fellow leftist Brooklynite. At one point, Ella Emhoff, the pro-Palestinian stepdaughter of Kamala Harris shared

---

8   Earlier in the steamy early summer day, Nixon posted a clip of herself walking to vote. She sported a t-shirt reading "Do Not Rank Cuomo," a popular refrain among several mayoral contenders. "I've never been so happy to vote for anyone," the former Cuomo challenger said, unironically.

a crowded staircase with Ossé. Everybody in the room festively sang "Hey, Hey Good-bye" to Cuomo.[9]

*

Across the East River, at the Carpenters Union Hall in lower Manhattan, Cuomo's people exited the room quickly after the toppled frontrunner conceded.

The veteran Democrat's "Potemkin campaign" needed strong support on election day but never assembled the volunteer operation to help make that happen. The whopping numbers of young and new voters that turned out during the initial nine days that ballots could be cast clearly signaled trouble for the former governor. Cuomo counted on the party's traditional base. Melissa de Rosa, his longtime aide and confidante with many female enemies—especially among the disgraced figure's thirteen sexual harassment accusers—appeared rather lonely as she passed out campaign lit near a poll site at Co-op City in the Bronx. Amid scorching heat on election day, the powerful figure once roundly accused of sending nursing home residents to die during the pandemic obliviously advised voters, "It is warm—but not too warm" to go vote.

Team Cuomo, as next-gen Democratic political consultant Nick Smith explained to Errol Louis on *Inside City Hall* on the night before primary day, had banked on the conventional wisdom that young as well as first-time voters would not show up at the polls. It was by no means the only stale,

---

9   *New York*'s David Freedlander (6-25-2025) labeled the supporter "Mamdaniacs."

cynical calculation made by Cuomo and his inept crew. At the union hall on Hudson Street, tragicomedy ensued. Shortly after the polls closed, Louis asked *Inside City Hall* reporter Ayana Harry if the people seen behind her seemed worn-out after doing election-day voter outreach in the heat. After thinking about it for a few seconds, Harry wryly observed that "their work was through writing checks."[10]

The downbeat mood at the Cuomo gathering was consistent with the dreary theme and messaging that the campaign had transmitted throughout the spring. According to the oh-so familiar candidate, New York City was experiencing a "crisis" of "disorder" that only someone with his decades of "experience" could "manage." A drop in crime numbers during the primary season undercut Cuomo's argument.

In his speech conceding the race, Cuomo's "thanks" to former mayor Michael Bloomberg, his leading billionaire backer, seemed sincere, but the former frontrunner's claims about his "special, talented" campaign staff rang hollow. With his three daughters—twins Cara and Mariah (b. 1995) and Andrea (b. 1997)—at his side, the aging pol (b. 1957) offered half-hearted praise for the "highly impactful campaign" run by his kids' peer. Mangling the pronunciation of Zohran's last name for the umpteenth

---

10 Northwestern University journalism professor Steven Thrasher, a former staff writer for the *Village Voice*, posted a video of the clip with him laughing hysterically at Harry's comment.

Run Zohran Run!

time, Cuomo acknowledged that "tonight is Assemblyman *Maan-donny*'s" night.[11]

When Cuomo asked the crowd to give Zohran a round of applause, a smattering of one-hand clapping echoed around the room.

*

Mamdani "is a communist at the highest level, and he wants to destroy New York," warned President Trump during a Fourth of July celebration in Des Moines, Iowa. "I love New York and we're not gonna let him do that," declared the Queens-born Don. As the U.S. celebrated its founding as a democracy, the second-edition president sounded like a vengeful, capricious monarch.

Earlier in the week, Trump—amplifying an incendiary attack made one month earlier by a far-right elected official from Queens—threatened to revoke Zohran's status as a naturalized U.S. citizen. When Councilwoman Vickie Paladino called for Mamdani's deportation in early June, the local response was notably muted. Led by candidates Brad Lander and Adrienne Adams, Mamdani's fellow contenders denounced Paladino, but the city's editorial boards and most other civic leaders remained silent.

---

11 After the first televised debate in early June, New York Communities for Change activist Pete Sikora, who has fought various Albany battles against the former governor, equated Cuomo's mispronunciations of Mamdani to Republicans' distortions of Kamala Harris' first name. "It's bigotry and signaling," Sikora tweeted on June 6.

Was the silence because Zohran is young, Muslim, pro-Palestine, a democratic socialist, or all four? The venom was often hard to sort out. As Cuomo backers launched what one longtime centrist city politics observer called "the most negative campaigning I have ever seen in my life!" both the *Times* and *New York Post* fanned the flames.[12] Although neither outlet endorsed Cuomo, both tried to kneecap Mamdani.

Zohran nevertheless made it through this trial by dumpster fire. Until the final three weeks of the campaign, Team Mamdani fought the blazes with very little outside support, even from many leftist figureheads. Although Rep. Rashida Tlaib, the nation's most prominent Palestinian American politician, had been in Mamdani's corner for months, AOC and Bernie did not weigh in until June. It was Mamdani and his devoted followers who stood at the front lines, holding steady amid an onslaught of hate.

While Cuomo fizzled, Zohran sizzled. That is the story of the 2025 mayoral primary in a nutshell. The how and why merit further scrutiny. Did the deluge of attacks funded by Bloomberg, Trumper Bill Ackman, and their fellow 1%-ers backfire? Zohran's stance on Israel was a recurring target in the over $26.5 million of outside money spent on Cuomo's behalf. Yet as Beinart surmised, many liberal Jews in New York City, and large numbers of all Democrats, do not support Israel's destruction of Gaza.

---

12   J.C. Polanco's June 29 televised remark (on WCBS) came in response to a pro-Cuomo consultant's ridiculous claim that "no one went negative against Mamdani."

Run Zohran Run!

Just four years earlier, the *New York Post* had been instrumental in Eric Adams' victory, while the *Times* helped Kathryn Garcia, a not-particularly charismatic novice politician, finish a very close second. This time around, the *Post* relentlessly trashed Mamdani, and the Bloomberg-allied *Times* treated the newcomer with absurdist condescension.

So who and what helped Zohran prevail? The roster is led by the DSA, which had propelled Mamdani's political career. Immediately after the October 7 Hamas attacks in Israel, powerful right-wing forces tried to crush the leftist group because of its robust support for Palestine. Less than two years later, a longtime DSA member defeated a very powerful mainstream Democrat. No explanation that minimizes the socialists' role in Zohran's success passes muster.

The list also includes activist groups such as Jewish Voice for Peace, Desis Rising, CAAAV, and NY Communities for Change. Millennial leaders like Asad Dandia, a Brooklyn-born Muslim with Pakistani roots, and numerous South Asian organizers such as Queens-based Felicia Singh helped mobilize their communities. From teenage first-time voters to AOC (b. 1989), Rep. Nydia Velázquez (b. 1953) and the socialist figurehead from Vermont (b. 1941), support for Mamdani spanned generations.

A former rapper, Zohran exuded plenty of charisma. His campaign's always stylish, often humorous use of social media made him a star. Mainstream outlets including the *New York Times*, *New York Post*, and *Politico* (New York) sought to shoot him down. But Zohran and company created their own stories, getting help from players not previously prominent in city politics, including the multi-platform media superstars Hasan Piker and Charlamagne Tha God.

As Zohran frequently phrased it before, during, and after primary day, his victory would close the books on the "politics of the past." The task of any historian is to explain how we arrived at a particular watershed moment. As we shall see, Mamdani succeeded largely because he represents a new generation of leaders—principled, uncompromising, and committed to innovative public policy—that knows how to craft their own narratives.

As our curtain rises, Eugene Debs—a.k.a. Bernie Sanders' hero—is about to step onto the stage.

PART ONE:
ORIGINS

CHAPTER 1
Cold War, R.I.P.

It's the middle of July 2024. Across the nation, the question is whether President Joe Biden will run for reelection. In New York City, local observers wonder if Mayor Eric Adams will face federal corruption charges. No matter whether that happens, the unpopular first-term mayor seems likely to face challengers in the June 2025 Democratic primary.

Committee members of the Democratic Socialists of America (DSA) chapter gather on a Saturday. According to journalist Peter Sterne, the activists "briefly discuss" something that has been "an open secret" within the DSA's ranks. One of the group's elected officials may challenge Adams. "DSA Assembly Member Zohran Mamdani is considering a run for mayor," announces the matter-of-fact headline in City & State, a publication read by political insiders.

Run Zohran Run!

By the end of the year, Mamdani is a social media star. As the race takes shape in the winter and spring of 2025, he consistently polls second in a crowded field. But the front-runner is not Mayor Adams, who—after cutting a deal with the Trump administration that ended the feds' corruption case—ducked out of the June Democratic primary in order to run as an independent in the general election.

Instead of an embattled incumbent mayor, Zohran now runs against a figure inextricably linked to a New York Democratic political dynasty. Although he had resigned as a thrice-elected governor amid a sexual harassment scandal in August 2021, Andrew Cuomo remains popular with older voters in the city. For many of Cuomo's key backers, the war in Gaza overshadows the problems faced by New York City. Mamdani's vocal support for Palestine becomes a lightning rod. Meanwhile, the genocide notwithstanding, Cuomo declares that he is "100% supportive of Israel."

Throughout the spring of 2025, Zohran's campaign gains growing momentum. The insurgent stands firm in support of Palestine and continues to call himself a democratic socialist. After his strong performance in the first televised debate, fellow DSA member Alexandria Ocasio-Cortez endorses Zohran, catapulting him into the national spotlight. Mamdani's sensational takedown of Cuomo in the second (and final) televised debate leads Brooklyn native Sen. Bernie Sanders, the elder statesman of democratic socialism in the U.S., to champion Zohran.

Mamdani handily defeats Cuomo in the June 24 primary. As the U.S. celebrates its 249th birthday, millions of younger voters no longer view socialism as un-American.[13]

*

In the first half of the twentieth century, socialism had plenty of currency in both national and New York politics. Starting in 1900, Eugene Debs ran for president five consecutive times, with four bids on the Socialist Party (SP) ballot line. In 1904 and 1908, his SP running mate was Ben Hanford, a labor leader in New York City.

In 1914, Debs' disciple Meyer London became the SP's second national member to win a seat in the House of Representatives,[14] defeating the powerful Tammany Hall (Democratic Party) candidate in a Lower East Side district. London, an outspoken opponent of President Woodrow Wilson's entry into World War I, served two terms until the Tammany machine candidate knocked him out in 1918. Two years later, London reclaimed his seat and served two more terms. London, a Jewish socialist, angered Zionists because he opposed "forcible annexation" in Palestine.

The 1920 election also saw five members of the Socialist Party win state assembly seats. As one historian explains,[15]

---

13 Note: Henceforth, citation information will be provided only for specific historical references or interpretations, not for quotes, news stories, podcasts, or social media statements posted on the internet during the campaign.
14 The first was Milwaukee's Victor Berger, elected in 1910.
15 Henry M. Greenberg in *Judicial Notice (*Spring 2012). Greenberg is the namesake in Greenberg Traurig, a powerhouse Albany law

all came from New York City districts with large populations of Russian Jews. Although the Democrats' assembly leader sought to form a coalition with the Socialist cadre (August Claessens, Samuel DeWitt, Samuel Orr, Charles Solomon, and Louis Waldman), Republican majority leader Thaddeus Sweet went on the warpath.

Sweet, a reactionary businessman from the Syracuse area, refused to seat the five Socialists, linking them to Bolshevism and denouncing their opposition to World War I. A few years after pushing the left out of Albany, the red-baiter won election to the House of Representatives. In 1928, Sweet became the first sitting member of Congress killed in an airplane crash.

Starting that same year, Norman Thomas, the New York City-based leader of the Socialist Party, ran for president in six consecutive elections. A pacifist until Pearl Harbor, Thomas frequently clashed with FDR. In advance of the 1936 election, Roosevelt encouraged his ally Mayor Fiorello La Guardia to work with union leaders in forming the American Labor Party (ALP), which aimed to shift Thomas' votes to FDR. David Dubinsky, leader of the International Ladies Garment Workers, characterized the union's 400,000 members as "all socialists," with more than half residing in New York City.[16]

---

firm that worked closely with then-Gov. Andrew Cuomo in his unsuccessful effort to stop DSA candidates in the 2020 New York state elections.

16   Theodore Hamm, *Bernie's Brooklyn* (OR Books, 2020), pp. 26-27.

A (very) liberal Republican who once won a race for Congress on the Socialist Party ballot line,[17] Mayor La Guardia's alliances with left-wing leaders including Vito Marcantonio caused critics to denounce the mayor as a red. In the 1940s, two members of the Communist Party—downtown Brooklyn's Pete Cacchione and Harlem's Ben Davis—held seats in the city council. In 1948, Davis and eleven of his comrades were charged and convicted of conspiracy to overthrow the federal government under the Smith Act. Like elsewhere in the U.S., the Cold War crackdown on radicalism effectively removed socialism from mainstream politics in New York.

*

Although socialism was no longer on the map, social democracy prevailed in New York City for the first few decades after World War II. The public provisions that greatly expanded under La Guardia—led by universal access to CUNY (which charged no tuition), and a low-cost health care network—remained intact through the early 1970s. During the same period, the city's Democratic Party maintained its New Deal orientation, remaining closely allied with large public sector unions.

As historian Kim Phillips-Fein explained in *Fear City* (2017), in response to the city's near-bankruptcy in 1975, Wall Street municipal bond traders created a blueprint that Democratic Governor Hugh Carey helped implement. That neoliberal agenda rolled back the city's large social

---

17 See Joshua B. Freeman's *Jacobin* profile of La Guardia (4-23-2025).

spending and sought to rein in the power of public sector unions.[18]

Media mogul Rupert Murdoch bought the *New York Post* in 1976, turning the previously liberal outlet into a right-wing attack machine. In 1977, Murdoch's support helped "tough-on-crime" Democrat Ed Koch capture City Hall. In his three terms (1978-89), Koch's neoliberal administration catered to Midtown real estate developers including Donald Trump. The future president also became a large donor to Governor Mario Cuomo, who was first elected in 1982, en route to a twelve-year reign.

None of Koch's successors—Democrat David Dinkins (1990-93), Republican Rudy Giuliani (1994-2001) or CEO Michael Bloomberg (2002-2013)—challenged the dominance of the FIRE (finance, insurance and real estate) sector. Bloomberg, a multi-billionaire, rose to influence as a FIRE product.[19] Outside of small leftist circles, socialism remained off the New York City political radar through the first decade of the 21st century.

In September 2011, Occupy Wall Street sprang up, with a large tent encampment remaining in the downtown financial district for several weeks. The movement was driven by the anarchist principles of mutual aid and solidarity, not by socialist demands for state-led redistribution of wealth.

---

18 Kim Phillips-Fein, *Fear City* (Metropolitan Books, 2017).
19 Robert Fitch's *The Assassination of New York* (Verso, 1996) remains the best work that examines the rise of the F.I.R.E.-dominated economy.

But Occupy's signature phrase, "We are the 99%," lent itself to various efforts.

Bill de Blasio, then the city's Public Advocate, visited the Occupy encampment. In the 2013 race for mayor, de Blasio ran as a progressive Democrat who called for taxing the rich in order to pay for universal pre-kindergarten (thus providing an economic benefit for parents because it reduced childcare costs). According to local political media outlets, de Blasio was the "Occupy" candidate in the race—which the movement's activists disputed.[20]

"A tale of two cities," de Blasio's Dickensian campaign theme, spotlighted the growth of inequality during the Bloomberg years. Joe Lhota, the Republican candidate in the general election, was clearly the preferred candidate of the 1%. "Mr. de Blasio's class warfare strategy in New York City," warned Lhota, was "straight out of the Marxist playbook." In response, de Blasio quipped "It's 2013," suggesting that socialism was a thing of the past.

When de Blasio crushed Lhota, the win was viewed as a liberal rejoinder to Bloomberg's "luxury city" model.[21] Few saw the next mayor as the new Fidel Castro. Once in office, de Blasio nevertheless successfully implemented universal pre-k (UPK), the city's largest social program expansion in recent memory. Governor Andrew Cuomo,

---

20 Brigid Bergin, WNYC (9-17-13); and Joe Coscarelli, *New York* (9-17-2013).
21 As Julian Brash explains, Bloomberg's administration viewed New York City as a "luxury brand," marketing it to prospective global investors in high-end real estate. Julian Brash, *Bloomberg's New York* (Univ. of Georgia, 2011).

de Blasio's nemesis and a close ally of the 1%, used existing state revenue to fund UPK—thus undercutting de Blasio's left-leaning campaign call for a targeted tax hike on millionaires.

The strong economy of the mid-2010s, driven in large part by low oil prices, allowed the progressive mayor to push through three consecutive years of rent freezes for the city's one million rent-regulated units.[22] In addition to the widespread economic benefits for public school parents and many tenants, de Blasio expanded the city government workforce and negotiated favorable contracts for most of the city's public sector unions.

By pushing popular New Deal-style initiatives, de Blasio cruised to reelection. Standoffish and unloved personally, de Blasio's policies nonetheless created solidly progressive legacies.

*

Mid-way through de Blasio's first term, Bernie Sanders brought socialism back into the national conversation. Although he characterized himself as a democratic socialist, most of Bernie's policies simply aligned with the New Deal. Sanders reminded his enthusiastic supporters that

---

[22] New York City's version of rent control is called rent stabilization. The mayor's appoints members of the Rent Guidelines Board (RGB), which determines the annual increase. Spikes in the yearly cost of heating oil in large rent-stabilized buildings are often a main factor in landlords' push for a yearly hike. Because the RGB members answer to the mayor, the size of the increase is widely seen as a reflection of the mayor's preference.

FDR "implemented a series of programs that put millions of people back to work, took them out of dire poverty and restored their faith in government." But "almost every program" FDR initiated was derided by his critics as "socialist," Bernie noted.

As his insurgent campaign gathered steam in early 2016, Sanders took aim at the "greed of Wall Street" at a speech in Midtown Manhattan. Even so, his proposed solution that day was to restore the Glass-Steagall regulations on the financial industry enacted during the New Deal—and eliminated by Wall Street-friendly Democrats including Chuck Schumer, with support from the Clinton White House.

Ahead of New York's presidential primary in April 2016, massive, mostly youthful crowds came out to see the septuagenarian socialist. Over 27,000 people heard Sanders denounce Wall Street in Washington Square, and a similar number of enthusiasts flocked to a Bernie rally in Brooklyn's Prospect Park.

One of Hillary Clinton's leading local supporters at the time was a rising star in the Democratic Party. In the words of Rep. Hakeem Jeffries, Sanders was simply "a gun-loving socialist with zero foreign policy experience." New York's mainstream Democrats forcefully repelled the insurgency, with Clinton easily winning the state primary by racking up large margins in the city.

The Sanders campaign nonetheless inspired a new generation of New York City leaders. "I started to call myself a socialist after Bernie's run in 2016," Zohran told

Jacobin's Liza Featherstone on the eve of his mayoral campaign launch.

Most New York City political observers paid little attention to Alexandria Ocasio-Cortez's primary challenge to longtime incumbent Queens congressman Joe Crowley in the spring of 2018. AOC, a member of the DSA, had volunteered for Bernie's 2016 campaign. Crowley, meanwhile, had served ten terms in Congress. He came from a well-known political family and was the leader of the large Queens Democratic Party organization.

Like most local media outlets,[23] the party establishment ignored the upstart campaign. When AOC pulled off the stunning upset in June, members of both camps attributed the win to the DSA's voter outreach strategy, which emphasized direct voter contact in the district that covers greater Astoria and Jackson Heights in Queens, and parts of the southern Bronx. "We knocked on their doors, we sent them mail, we knocked on their doors again, we called them," explained Corbin Trent, AOC's communications director at the time.[24]

AOC, like Bernie, advocated Medicare for All, free college tuition, and campaign finance reform. Along with the DSA, she would soon push for a Green New Deal, further illustrating the alignment between contemporary democratic socialists and FDR's legacy. AOC's mastery of social media

---

23 *The Indypendent* was a notable exception. Its June 2018 print issue featured AOC on its cover and copies were widely circulated in Northwest Queens.
24 *City & State* (6-27-2018).

soon made her a national figure. The Democratic Party's neoliberal leadership neither embraced the rising star nor championed any of her policies.

In the wake of AOC's surprise success, the local chapter of the DSA focused on New York races in the fall 2018 statewide elections. The first of the group's several wins also previewed the main conflict it would confront in the mid-2020s.

Like AOC, the DSA's Julia Salazar sought to topple an entrenched legislator. State Senator Martin Dilan had represented fast-gentrifying Bushwick, Brooklyn, for sixteen years. Rather than focus on Salazar's calls for universal rent control or sex worker rights, local media outlets highlighted her stance on Israel.

Salazar's support for BDS—the movement calling for boycotts and divestments from Israel, which Gov. Andrew Cuomo had tried to squash—and Palestinian rights produced a relentless stream of attacks, with questions raised about her Jewish identity. The insurgent campaign carried the backing of Jews for Racial and Economic Justice, a pro-Palestine group for which Salazar had worked for as an organizer.[25]

DSA ground troops helped propel their candidate to a comfortable victory (59-41%) in the September primary, further angering Israel hawks. An opinion piece headline in the *New York Times* labeled Salazar as "the left's

---

25   Charles Dunst, *Jewish Telegraphic Agency* (8-23-2018).

post-truth politician." The commentator, not surprisingly, was militant Zionist Bari Weiss.[26]

In the wake of Mamdani's triumph in the 2025 primary, NYC-DSA co-chair Grace Mausser noted that an unsuccessful 2019 campaign supported by the group actually paid long-term dividends. In the Democratic primary for Queens district attorney, Tiffany Cabán, a public defender in her early thirties running on a radical platform calling for decarceration, nearly defeated 54-year-old centrist Melinda Katz, the party machine candidate.

Zohran and many of his fellow future supporters worked on the Cabán campaign, which captured national attention because the race took place amid the peak of the criminal justice reform movement. After Cabán lost by only sixty votes in a borough-wide race, Mausser explained six years later, the city's DSA chapter realized that it had the potential to win big electoral prizes.[27] The DSA's Tascha Van Auken served as Zohran for NYC's field director, and the cadre's dedicated members spurred the campaign's dynamic field operation.

*

In the spring of 2019, Bernie Sanders launched his second presidential run with a kickoff event at Brooklyn College, which he attended in the late 1950s before transferring to the University of Chicago. While reiterating his key policy

---

26 Bari Weiss, *New York Times* (9-14-2018).
27 "If we only had only knocked on 60 more doors...," Mausser lamented on a DSA post-primary Zoom call (June 30).

proposals from the 2016 campaign, Bernie pledged to fight for "economic justice, social justice, racial justice, and environmental justice." He also praised New York City's rent control protections, explaining that they provided stability for his lower middle-class family while he grew up near Brooklyn College.

Although he simply advocated New Deal policies, Sanders' self-identification as a socialist continued to raise hackles. After Bernie became the early frontrunner, Joe Biden warned in a televised debate that the label of "democratic socialist" would hurt Sanders if he became the nominee. ABC moderator George Stephanopoulos, a longtime Clintonite, then asked the other candidates if they were "concerned about having a democratic socialist at the top of the ticket."

After the debate, MSNBC host Chris Matthews ludicrously compared Bernie to Fidel Castro and warned that a Sanders win would result in "executions in Central Park." Just before Super Tuesday, *60 Minutes* host Anderson Cooper grilled Bernie regarding his past praise of Castro. Meanwhile, Michael Bloomberg entered the race and started spending enormous sums (eventually exceeding $1 billion) of his own money in order to help sink Bernie. The coordinated assault of Democratic Party leaders and their corporate media allies helped sink Sanders again.

2020 was nonetheless a banner year for DSA candidates in New York. In central Brooklyn, Jabari Brisport won a state senate seat, and Phara Souffrant Forrest toppled an incumbent Hakeem Jeffries-ally in the state assembly. Democratic socialist Marcela Mitaynes knocked out a veteran Cuomo-linked assemblymember in Brooklyn's Sunset Park.

In northern Queens, Mamdani and Jessica González-Rojas made it four wins for the insurgent group's assembly candidates. In a congressional district that included the northern Bronx and suburban Westchester County, DSA-backed Jamaal Bowman toppled 16-term incumbent Eliot Engel, one of the Democrats' leading Israel hawks. All of the 2020 democratic socialist winners cruised to reelection two years later.

Along with Cabán, who won a council seat in Astoria, Queens, the DSA's Alexa Avilés triumphed in Brooklyn's Sunset Park and Red Hook in the 2021 New York City races. Four years later, Mamdani and Avilés (b. 1973, making her about twenty years older than most of her fellow democratic socialist elected officials) frequently campaigned together, helping the incumbent councilwoman defeat a primary challenger funded largely by Bibi's backers.

After the October 7 attacks, Jamaal Bowman's statements in support of a ceasefire and Palestinian rights put him in the crosshairs. Democratic Majority for Israel, an AIPAC-aligned national organization, targeted Bowman, whose district had been redrawn to include more suburbanites. In the 2024 Democratic primary, George Latimer, a veteran nonentity from Westchester, captured the support of pro-Israel voters and defeated Bowman. The unseated Congressman played an active role during the final month of Zohran's primary campaign, helping Mamdani gain votes in the Bronx.

By 2025, the DSA's ranks of statewide elected officials included three senators and seven members of the state assembly. The national group was no longer allied with AOC, although the New York City chapter continued to back her. That conflict involved her statements regarding Israel, not questions about AOC's commitment to democratic socialism.

*

Like the rest of the Democratic Party establishment, Andrew Cuomo views socialism as a term of derision. In mid-May 2025, as the late June primary began to heat up, Cuomo explained his view of the DSA to the *Times of Israel*. "I don't consider them Democrats," the former governor said. "I consider them socialists."

Unnerved by Mamdani's momentum as primary day neared, the *New York Times* editorial board denigrated the candidate in two much-discussed opinion pieces. In summarizing the views of the mayoral candidates among the "experts" on a panel of fifteen influential New Yorkers, the board explained that Cuomo's "heavy baggage" and Mamdani's "image as a democratic socialist" accounted for why each received only two first-place rankings.

One member of the *Times* panel who supported Cuomo nonetheless was impressed by Mamdani. According to veteran NYU public policy professor Mitchell Moss, the DSA candidate was "not speaking to just poor people; he's speaking to young people who are not poor, but they feel he's talking to them." "Unfortunately," Moss continued, Mamdani is "basically running a Bernie Sanders local version."

Four days after presenting the expert panel recommendations, the *Times* implored voters not to rank the insurgent. Mamdani, declared the editorial board, "is a democratic socialist who too often ignores the unavoidable trade-offs of governance."

Meanwhile, as Zohran's run gained steam earlier in the spring, the far-right *New York Post* called the DSA candidate's plan for free busses "something out of the Politburo." As I pointed out at the time in the *Indypendent*, the twentieth-century reference was likely only something that registered for the tabloid's longtime readers, many of whom ride the Staten Island Ferry back and forth to Manhattan for...free.

On Sunday, June 22, red-baiting figured prominently in Cuomo's last pitch to voters ahead of the Tuesday primary. At the Christian Cultural Center, a very large Black church in Brooklyn, the former governor warned an older audience that "there is a far-left movement taking over the Democratic Party," referring to the DSA. The city was at a "tipping point," he declared. Cuomo, unwittingly, was correct.

The jittery frontrunner also addressed the electrical workers union's Catholic Council in Midtown Manhattan that morning. Neither "the MAGA right" nor the "democratic socialist left" have agendas that "include us," Cuomo told a friendly crowd made up of aging white labor officials. The reactionary Democratic Party establishment was imploding.

On the day after his humiliating primary defeat, Cuomo spoke at length to his preferred reporter, WCBS-TV mainstay Marcia Kramer.[28] "'Everything free' sounds good—free busses, free groceries" is how the former governor caricatured Mamdani's appeal. A chorus of naysayers derided Mamdani's proposal for "government-run grocery stores" as some sort of Soviet-style rationing. Somehow the creation of low-cost (i.e. not free) supermarkets, an initiative seen in cities across the U.S., did not compute for lifelong New York Democrats like Cuomo.

Mayor Adams, a former Republican turned right-wing Democrat, piled on. On the day after the primary, he met with the *New York Post*'s far-right editorial board, which helped elect Adams four years earlier. The mayor dutifully labeled Mamdani a "snake-oil salesman" for a "socialist city."

A button-pushing bigot whose default move is to play the race card, Adams then unironically insisted that the "young, white voters" who support Mamdani "don't even know what socialism is."

The final primary tallies showed that Mamdani scored over 50% more first place votes than Adams received

---

28 Kramer, now in her mid-seventies, is generally the go-to reporter for the city elite and hostile to progressives. But when she sat down with Mamdani in March, her questions were not at all hard-hitting. One likely factor in Kramer's decision-making is that Cuomo was comfortably ahead in the polls at the time.

four years earlier. A millennial, Muslim disciple of Bernie Sanders completely flummoxed the New York City elite, which had long assumed that the twin pillars of their worldview—that capitalism is sacrosanct, and Israel must never be criticized—would remain unchallenged.

Whether Mamdani's proposals amounted to actual socialism or were simply extensions of New Deal liberalism was a debate too academic for the mayoral candidates or most mainstream media commentators to even consider. As we will see in the chapters ahead, Zohran upended the status quo in myriad ways.

For now, let's note that June 24, 2025, marked the full-fledged return of the S-word to mainstream New York City politics.

CHAPTER 2

Roots

"I am an Indian-Ugandan New Yorker," Zohran once said. "It's the hyphenated immigrant dream."[29]

Born October 18, 1991, in Kampala, Zohran Kwame Mamdani spent the first five years of his life in Uganda. Kampala, the nation's capital, was then a modest-sized city, with a population just under one million.

Mahmood Mamdani's ancestors were Gujarati Muslims who left the coastal region northwest of Mumbai in the late nineteenth century, journeying across the Arabian Sea through the Indian Ocean first to Tanzania, later moving to neighboring Uganda. By the end of the twentieth century, over two million people of Indian descent lived in Africa, mainly in the continent's southeastern nations.

---

29 Unless otherwise noted, the quotes from Zohran in this chapter come from two 90-minute interviews the author conducted with Mamdani in the early spring of 2025.

Run Zohran Run!

Bhubaneswar, located in the northeast India state of Odisha, was a very small town (pop. under 50,000) when Mira Nair grew up there in the 1960s, in a Hindu household. After earning a B.A. from Harvard, Nair started making films in what was then called Bombay (now Mumbai). In 1988, she visited Uganda while doing research for *Mississippi Masala*, her 1991 Hollywood debut that starred Denzel Washington. While in Kampala, she met Mahmood Mamdani.

When nationalist dictator Idi Amin took power in 1972, he forced all South Asians to leave Uganda, sending the Mamdani family to refugee centers in London. "My grandfather was forever changed by the expulsion," Zohran explains. In Uganda, his grandfather had been a manager at a cotton ginnery and held other comparable positions while also writing poetry.

While in London, Zohran noted, his grandparents "would go to Gatwick every week and watch planes take off back to Uganda, wishing that they were on them. What was taken from them was a sense of self, a sense of stability, and a sense of belonging."

Among the insights that Zohran gained from his family's plight is that "It taught me the lasting impacts of being displaced—whether it's caused by an expulsion or an eviction."

In the 1970s, Idi Amin was a familiar presence in U.S. popular culture, quite memorably spoofed by Richard Pryor, the legendary radical comedian.[30] It's hard to

---

30 *Saturday Night Live*'s Garrett Morris also played Amin in several skits in the late 1970s.

imagine that anyone predicted at the time that Amin's legacy might one day influence New York City politics.

*

Mahmood Mamdani was among the small number of South Asians who returned after Amin's downfall in 1979. As he noted in a 2022 essay in the *London Review of Books*, after Amin was overthrown, Mahmood went back to Uganda, where he was a citizen. After first interning for a Christian organization, he next took a position at Kampala's Makerere University in 1980.

After spending his first five years in the Ugandan capital, Zohran lived for two years in South Africa, where his father taught at the University of Cape Town. This meant that in his youth, Zohran lived in a nation governed by South Africa's first democratically elected president, Nelson Mandela, who was in office from 1994 to 1999.

Zohran's family moved to the U.S. in 1999, when Prof. Mamdani was named the Herbert H. Lehman Professor of Government at Columbia University. An only child, Zohran lived with his parents in faculty housing near the Columbia campus in Morningside Heights. The family frequently traveled back to Uganda.

Upon moving to the city, Zohran attended Bank Street, a progressive private school near Columbia. Zohran fondly recalls his favorite teachers and said that Bank Street "provided a very nurturing and loving environment." On the morning of the September 11 attacks, a teacher named

Stephanie[31] pulled the 9-year-old aside and told him that if he got bullied because he was a Muslim, Zohran should let her know.

"That was the opposite experience of most Muslim kids in the city at the time," Zohran observes. "I was lucky to have the teacher that I did."

In general, Zohran does not recall many direct encounters with Islamophobia on the streets of New York City while growing up. However, in the spring of 2008, after his return from one of his trips to Uganda, Zohran said that he was detained at JFK and taken into a double-mirrored room with other Muslim men. Homeland Security agents then asked if he had visited a terrorist training camp.

It was a brief, but scary experience for the teenager. "I was terrified," Zohran recalls.

In the aftermath of his primary win, billionaire Bill Ackman, the pro-Israel zealot who helped fuel the crackdown on pro-Palestine protests at campuses including Columbia, distorted Mahmood Mamdani's explanation of Al-Qaeda's adherents in order make it seem like both Mamdanis support the 9/11 terrorist attacks. The *New York Post* amplified Ackman's smear.

As Muslims gain political power in the city, the disease of Islamophobia lingers.

*

---

31 In the New York City public schools, grade-school teachers (and paraprofessionals) are typically called "Miss" or "Mister" followed by their first name, but Bank Street had a more informal protocol.

"I would take the 1 train uptown to W. 231st Street, ride the BX10 bus, and yell 'back door!'" is how Zohran recalls his daily commute from Morningside Heights to high school in the northcentral Bronx. Along with Stuyvesant, Brooklyn Tech, and a handful of others, Bronx Science (or just "Science," as Zohran refers to it) is one of New York City elite public high schools, requiring a specialized admission test.

Zohran's favorite teacher at Science was Marc Kagan, a former transit workers union official who made a late-career transition to education. The older brother of SCOTUS justice Elena Kagan taught social studies. As Zohran recalled, "One of the lessons Kagan imparted is that intelligence means nothing without the application of it."

Kagan introduced students to pedagogy. Seniors in his Advanced Placement world history class taught a specific lesson to each of the three class years below them. Kagan thus "showed just how difficult it is to capture the imagination—let alone the attention—of teenage students," Mamdani explains.

It will come as no surprise that Zohran joined Science's prestigious debate team as a freshman. But he did not stay long because he wanted to play soccer, eventually becoming the school's goal-scoring team captain in his senior year. Mamdani's favorite player at the time was Thierry Henry, the graceful French forward who starred for Arsenal in the Premier League through 2007.[32]

---

32 Zohran's favorite bands as a teen included Franz Ferdinand, Artic Monkeys and Kaiser Chiefs. In 2002, Mahmood and son saw

Run Zohran Run!

As the mayoral contender informed Vulture's Nicholas Quah, "I came up as a fan in the early 2000s, and it was my uncle who introduced me to the team. Arsenal was one of the first teams to have a number of African players: Lauren, Kolo Toure, Nwankwo Kanu, Emmanuel Eboue, Alex Song. As an Ugandan kid looking at this team, I was just so proud."

Zohran told me that he remains an "obsessive Arsenal fan." At a pre-canvassing rally in Bed-Stuy during the last month of the primary, Mamdani spotted an eleven-year-old boy named Vic wearing an Arsenal jersey. The candidate came over to chat with the lad about the pair's favorite squad, making Vic very excited about Zohran's run.

While at Science, Mamdani co-founded a cricket club, which soon became part of a citywide, twelve-team, public high school league. As the Science squad traveled across the city, Zohran recalled, "I was getting a tour of the South Asian diaspora—playing teams that were Bangladeshi, Pakistani, Guyanese, Trinidadian, etc."

When asked to describe his level of skill, Zohran laughs. "In cricket, typically a player either excels as a batsman or a bowler. I tried to do both. I was good but not great. But there are very few feelings like when you bowl someone out, or when you hit a four or a six—and these were thrilling moments in my high school career."

Egyptian legend Hakim perform with Algerian powerhouse Khaled at the Beacon Theatre.

As the son of a leading political theorist, Zohran was encouraged to pay attention to world affairs while growing up. During Obama's 2008 campaign, the teenager rode on a bus full of volunteer doorknockers to central Pennsylvania. The future politician recalls liking Obama at the time because of the candidate's opposition to the Iraq War.

In his junior year at Science, Zohran ran for vice president and lost by a wide margin. The bid marked his debut as a rapper, as he cut a video in support of his campaign. For his AP literature class in his senior year, Mamdani and a classmate traded lines over an instrumental version of "Still Dre." It would be an exaggeration to say that Zohran was a prodigy by the end of high school. But the worldly lad clearly had skills, potential, and plenty of ambition.

*

Shortly after his shocking win in the 2025 primary, the *New York Times* embarrassed itself by creating a scandal about Zohran's college application to Columbia. The teenager who grew up in an Indian household in Uganda checked the boxes for Asian and African American. That is not how Mamdani has identified himself since becoming a public figure, rendering the substance of the story minimal at most.

The controversy nevertheless lit up the internet over the Fourth of July weekend, with liberal *Times* columnist Jamelle Bouie siding with the paper's many critics. The sources of the hit piece were known eugenicists and white nationalist stalking horses. Breaking its own ethics rules, the *Times* used hacked documents without initially identifying the direct source of the info, even though that far-right figure was known to the outlet.

After his rejection from Columbia, Zohran attended Bowdoin College in Brunswick, Maine, where he majored in Africana Studies. His favorite professor was Brian Purnell, a leading scholar of Brooklyn during the civil rights era. One of Purnell's courses used David Simon's classic series *The Wire* (2002-2008) as a point of entry to discuss urban political economy. It was an eye-opener, according to Zohran.

Purnell recalls that Mamdani "enjoyed talking about discussions and debates from our courses outside of class time. He also had a wonderful sense of humor and brought joy and fun to the serious issues that we studied."[33] The future mayoral candidate's courses with Purnell covered subjects including the history of Reconstruction in the U.S. and the historical legacy of racial slavery. Bowdoin is 875 miles, but light years away, from Michigan's Hillsdale College, the center of MAGA-approved U.S. history.

Zohran's senior research project focused on Frantz Fanon's classic works *Black Skin, White Masks* and *The Wretched of the Earth*. As Purnell, his advisor, notes, Mamdani "compared Fanon's theories on colonialism and anti-colonialism to Rousseau and Enlightenment political philosophies on the 'social contract.'" In his favorite professor's view, the Fanon project "showcased how

---

33 Quotes are from Purnell's 7-7-2025 email to author.

dynamic and broad Zohran's mind was when he was an undergraduate student."

While at Bowdoin, Zohran co-founded a chapter of Students for Justice in Palestine. After his 2025 primary victory, the *New York Post* reported that in November 2013, the Bowdoin chapter invited radical Lebanese scholar As'ad AbuKhalil to speak at the campus. AbuKhalil's argument that the 9/11 attacks were blowback from the actions of the US is a perspective shared by a range of commentators, including ex-CIA consultant Chalmers Johnson. But the *Post*, predictably, presented this as tantamount to support for Osama bin Laden.

Zohran completed his undergraduate degree in 2014. "I don't think that Zohran's studies at Bowdoin had a direct influence on his political career," Purnell observes. "But without question they helped him develop deep ideas related to justice, democracy, and the common good, all of which shape his current approach to public service."

*

After college, Zohran went to Uganda, where he developed his rap career. "Young Cardamom" (YC) as he first called himself, teamed up with his childhood pal Hussein Abdul Bar, or HAB, a Black Ugandan. "Kanda (Chap Chap)," a video posted on YouTube in September 2015, shows the duo travel around the outskirts of Kampala in a small flatbed cart pulled by a motorcycle.

Alternately wearing casual and traditional African clothing, YC and Hab distribute free chapati (the "chap" repeated in the song), which is the same as roti but made with a Ugandan plantain called matooke. Just after the midway point of the 4-minute clip, the rappers switch into college graduation attire. They then lecture to—and dance with—a group of Black graduates who receive a rolled-up chapati as a diploma.

Upbeat and cross-cultural, Young Cardamom and HAB soon reached audiences across the globe. In 2016, *OkayAfrica*, the popular arts and lifestyle news site based in Brooklyn, interviewed the duo. As Zohran stated, "we rap in six different languages—Luganda, English, Hindi, Swahili, Runyoro, and Nubi. People don't associate all these languages with Kampala, but for the two of us, Kampala cannot simply be lived in Luganda or English."[34] Zohran's linguistic range surpasses that of Fiorello La Guardia, New York City's last polyglot mayor.[35]

When Mamdani discusses his music career in Kampala, he is often self-deprecating. "When you're the warm-up act to the warm-up act, you learn humility," he maintains. It seems more likely that he and his partner had at least a decent-sized following in Uganda.

The duo's prominence grew upon the release of Mira Nair's *Queen of Katwe*, which premiered at the Toronto Film Festival in September 2016. YC and HAB recorded

---

34 *OkayAfrica* (5-12-2016).
35 La Guardia (1882-1947) was raised in a Jewish-Italian household (in Greenwich Village) and spoke Yiddish, Italian, German, and Croatian. On the 2025 trail, Mamdani also made headlines by speaking fluent Spanish.

"Spice," the film's lead number, then released a video of that track featuring Kenya-raised actress Lupita Nyong'o, who was then en route to international stardom.

Now in his mid-twenties, Zohran was splitting his time between Kampala and Manhattan. In 2017, he started working in New York City politics. From his parents' home in Morningside Heights, Zohran rode the subway all the way to Bay Ridge at the southern end of Brooklyn. On a weekday, that's at least a one-hour ride, and on a weeknight it's closer to ninety minutes.

As many New Yorkers will unhappily remember, 2017 was known locally as the "summer of hell," when the MTA's aging infrastructure crumbled. It was more notable when any subway ride was *not* delayed. The resulting packed subway cars must have been especially challenging for people like Zohran, who describes himself as "quite claustrophobic."

How Mamdani dealt with the compounded hardship catalyzed his future success. During the unending delays, with the train cars stalled in the tunnels, the 25-year-old asked strangers around him on the subway cars for help. "I would start by telling people that I am claustrophobic and spiraling," he recalls. "Then I'd say, 'Would you mind if we chat for a few minutes until the train starts moving?'"

"People humored me," continues Zohran. "And they were very kind. It was a quite difficult time, but I still rode the subway every day. It was definitely a memorable experience." The budding leader found strength in his fellow city dwellers.

Run Zohran Run!

Solidarity among working people became the essence of Zohran's 2025 run. Candidates who drive to the office cannot directly relate to the shared experience of millions of subway commuters.

*

What brought Zohran to Bay Ridge was the inspired city council campaign of Khader El-Yateem (b. 1968), who was raised in Palestine. A Lutheran minister and DSA member, El-Yateem's candidacy mobilized voters in Bay Ridge's sizable Palestinian community. The candidate's life story, which included an arrest by Israel on political grounds, impressed Mamdani.

In the primary that September, progressive Democrat Justin Brannan defeated El-Yateem 39-31%, with three others in the race. "He is a principled fighter for human rights," Zohran said about El-Yateem, who has since moved to Florida.

Zohran returned to Bay Ridge in 2018, this time to manage left-liberal journalist Ross Barkan's run for a state senate in the Democratic primary. Barkan, who describes himself as an "Israel-skeptical Jew," recalled in a June 2025 Substack essay that Zohran put up a poster of Mo Salah, the Liverpool star, in their campaign office.

According to Barkan, his energetic campaign manager's "philosophy" was that "you did not sit down." Although the spirited bid fell short, Zohran was increasingly prepared to run for office.

Mamdani next went to work for Chhaya, an economic empowerment organization that serves South Asian and

Indo-Caribbean communities in Queens, with offices in Jackson Heights and Richmond Hill. As a foreclosure prevention counselor, Zohran's salary before he entered the state assembly was $47,000. He now moved into a rent-stabilized one-bedroom apartment in Astoria, which is still his residence. As of mid-2025, the rent was $2,300 per month.[36]

"Home," stated Zohran, "is a through-line of my work. At Chhaya, the question was 'how do we keep people in their homes'? Now, my campaign is asking 'how do we keep people in the city that they call home?'"

In his spare time while working at Chhaya, Zohran continued developing his music career. In 2019, Zohran recorded another memorable rap video. Now known as "Mr. Cardamom," the performer teamed up with popular South Asian actress Madhur Jaffrey (b. 1933, in Delhi). The song is called "Nani" (grandmother), with Jaffrey as the title character. Wearing an apron but shirtless, Mr. Cardamom raps from inside a crowded halal food truck.

When the video debuted, the *New York Times* gave it a favorable write-up in the outlet's popular food section (Jaffrey is also known for her cookbooks). Playful photos showed a beaming Zohran and the feisty actress in the aisles of Patel Brothers, a longstanding South Asian grocery store in Jackson Heights.

Six years later, the same powerful media outlet tried to burst Zohran's balloon.

---

36 The current salary for New York state legislators is $142,000.

CHAPTER 3
Roti and Roses

Zohran's journey to City Hall began in Astoria. In 2020, he unseated a Democratic incumbent in the state assembly district that covered the Northwest Queens neighborhood as well as adjacent Long Island City. By that point, non-DSA elected officials had already acknowledged that the leftist group held a firm grip on Astoria politics.

Soon after he started working for Chhaya, Zohran started volunteering for DSA-backed Tiffany Cabán's 2019 bid for Queens district attorney. Raised in a Puerto Rican household in Richmond Hill, a central Queens area in which Mamdani then worked as a foreclosure counselor, Cabán (b. 1987) was a public defender in Manhattan when she ran for DA as a first-time candidate.

At the time of Tiffany's campaign, Zohran, who grew up in upper-middle-class household, was helping struggling working-class families, while Cabán, who came from a working-class household, understood the hardships faced by underclass communities ensnared in the criminal justice system. Public school teachers and sundry nonprofit sector workers similarly filled the NYC-DSA's ranks, with many of the activists sharing Mamdani's socioeconomic background.

In order to win a race in a borough with 2.3 million residents, the socialist cadre needed to partner with community groups and leaders across Queens. In the process, the NYC-DSA built a network of allies for future campaigns, propelling both Zohran's 2020 run for state assembly and his bid for mayor five years later.

*

Via his work with Chhaya, Zohran became familiar with Jackson Heights, which had been known for decades as a South Asian neighborhood; and Richmond Hill, which has a fast-growing South Asian and Indo-Caribbean population. As he told *Jacobin*'s Hadas Thier two years later, Mamdani became "a DSA point person" for Cabán's campaign, serving as a field organizer in these locations.

In sync with the then-growing national movement for criminal justice reform, Cabán advanced a decarceral agenda that radically challenged the status quo. The AOC-backed candidate called for shorter felony sentences, vowed not to prosecute nonviolent offenses (including sex work), and pledged to hold bad landlords accountable.

The primary contest went into overtime, with ballots counted by hand and challenged in court. Zohran was a committed volunteer, observing the post-primary day proceedings on behalf of the campaign. Cabán's narrow defeat (by 60 votes) initiated a power struggle between the Northwest Queens-based DSA and Rep. Gregory Meeks, the Queens Democratic Party boss based in Southeast Queens, an area with many Black homeowners.

As Mamdani explained to Thier, a DSA colleague then encouraged him to run for the assembly seat held by progressive Democrat Aravella Simotas, a five-term incumbent whose Greek heritage corresponded with Astoria's previous neighborhood identity. Zohran criticized Simotas for being too close to the Queens Democratic Party brass, citing her support for county leader Joe Crowley during AOC's 2018 run. The incumbent also did not endorse Cabán.

Zohran's anti-machine messaging drew criticism from Assemblywoman Catalina Cruz, a liberal Democrat who represents the neighboring district. As Cruz told *City & State*'s Rebecca Lewis, the Meeks-led county organization "no longer had power" in Astoria. Cruz (b. 1979) backed Simotas (b. 1978) and neither figure seemed to grasp why Mamdani appealed to his fellow millennials.

The socialist candidate celebrated his Indian-Ugandan heritage, frequently wearing long South Asian shirts called kurtas and including his African middle name on the ballot. The former rapper's "roti and roses" platform playfully updated the old socialist slogan, matching a South Asian staple with the DSA's red flower symbol. The spicy insurgent toppled the bland Simotas by a margin of just under 425 votes.

Cynthia Nixon plugged Zohran in *The Nation* in late January 2020, introducing readers to Mamdani and the rest of the NYC-DSA's slate in that year's state elections. The roster included future State Senator Jabari Brisport and victorious assemblymembers Phara Souffrant Forrest and Marcela Mitaynes. *Jacobin* and the *Indypendent* also paid close attention to Mamdani's first run.

By the end of 2020, Zohran's political career was on the ascent. 8,410 primary voters in Astoria and Long Island City, including the candidate himself, had no idea how fast Zohran would rise. Five years later, nearly a half-million other New York Democrats came out in support of the next-generation socialist.

*

Scores of Cabán campaign volunteers worked closely with the DSA but did not belong to the group. Felicia Singh is a prominent community organizer in Ozone Park, a neighborhood close to JFK Airport with a large South Asian and Indo-Caribbean population. Now in her mid-thirties, Felicia grew up in Ozone Park. Her mother is a Guyanese Muslim and her father is a Sikh Punjabi—a distinctly "new Queens" mix.

As Felicia explains, after volunteering for Cabán, she went door-to-door as a 2020 Census taker. She then ran for City Council in 2021, winning the Democratic primary with a platform focused on education issues, transportation, and climate resiliency (low-lying communities in Queens have faced severe flooding in recent years). Because polyglot Ozone Park is in the same district as Howard Beach, a bastion of ethnic white conservatism, a Republican defeated Singh in the general election.

Theodore Hamm

Singh led a number of canvass teams for Mamdani's 2025 primary campaign, covering Ozone Park, South Ozone Park, and adjacent Richmond Hill. Whether Sikh, Hindu, or Muslim, most South Asian voters identified with Zohran because "he looks like them," Felicia told me in early July.

"We really started laying the groundwork for Zohran's success in 2019," Singh added. As noted in earlier chapter, NYC-DSA co-chair Grace Mausser similarly viewed the Cabán campaign as a catalyst. In the 2019 campaign season with few other races on the ballot, the leftists' borough-wide candidate reeled in just under 35,000 votes, so winning a citywide contest remained a tall order. But in the wake of his successful assembly run, Mamdani's name recognition steadily grew.

After entering the state legislature, Zohran became a familiar presence at Palestinian solidarity events organized by Jewish Voice for Peace. In May 2021, the legislator addressed fifty or so activists gathered at Brooklyn's Grand Army Plaza, which is directly across from Sen. Chuck Schumer's home.

"I have been called a terrorist," stated a beardless Mamdani while holding a microphone and standing on the base of a flagpole. "I have been called an antisemite...[But] there is something we all know here that must be spoken: anti-Zionism is not antisemitism." As the crowd cheers him on, Mamdani then loudly declares, "In the anti-Zionism I believe in there is NO ROOM for antisemitism."[37]

---

37 See video shot by Javier Soriano: https://www.youtube.com/watch?v=0wh1ds2Lwcg&t=2356s

Run Zohran Run!

It is not clear whether the powerful Israel ally who lives across the street from Grand Army Plaza heard Zohran that Friday evening. But soon after October 7, Mamdani returned—and Chuck was not at all thrilled to see him.

*

In the fall of 2021, Zohran impressed many South Asian city residents by joining a hunger strike on behalf of taxi drivers experiencing a debt crisis spurred by predatory lenders. Over the preceding few years, several bankrupted South Asian taxi medallion holders had committed suicide.

The crisis dated back to the Bloomberg administration, when the medallions required for licensed taxis reached inflated levels that required drivers to take steep loans. The city then allowed Uber and other for-hire vehicles to flood the streets, thus deflating the value of the medallions. The de Blasio administration faced a stream of criticism over its insufficient relief assistance to the indebted drivers.

Along with left-aligned assemblymember Yuh-Line Niou, who at the time represented nearby Chinatown, Zohran joined many drivers in a fifteen-day hunger strike outside City Hall starting in mid-October 2021. The legislators did so in solidarity with the Taxi Workers Alliance (TWA), which had been pushing a comprehensive debt relief plan for months. When the de Blasio administration finally agreed to enact the TWA plan in early November, Zohran, Yuh-Line, and drivers across the city celebrated.

"We can have a future!!" fellow hunger striker Augustine Tang texted to a *City & State* reporter. Tang also noted that he had been experiencing headaches, chills, and hunger pangs. Zohran told the same outlet that this was by no means his first time going without food.

"I'm Muslim, and I fast during Ramadan," Zohran noted. The activist-lawmaker noted that a date is the first thing he typically consumes at the end of the ritual. As the taxi worker protest concluded, Zohran, and Yuh-Line consumed a date and scoops of avocado.

Zohran added that breaking the fast outside of City Hall "alongside my elders [and] people who've been fighting this issue for years" gave him "a profound appreciation of the joys and the dignity of food. And I don't think I'll ever look at an avocado or a date the same."[38]

Less than four years later, Mamdani was ready to move inside the building.[39]

*

Although the events of October 7, 2023, occurred 5,700 miles away, shockwaves instantly rippled across New York City. The violent attack by Hamas was the first incursion ever by Palestinian forces into Israel-held territory. Nearly 1,200 Israelis were killed, including 736 civilians. Hamas seized roughly 250 hostages.

---

38 *City & State* (11-4-2021).
39 During Ramadan in March 2025, Zohran for NYC posted a well-received YouTube video in which Mamdani and Kareem Rahma, a popular Egyptian American Muslim comedian, discuss the candidate's advocacy for taxi workers with a cabbie from Côte d'Ivoire named Mouhamadou. Zohran and Mouhamadou participated in the hunger strike.

Run Zohran Run!

New York's disparate antiwar groups quickly called for a protest in Times Square on Sunday, October 8. Neither the national nor local DSA co-sponsored the event. But what happened that day caused pols and pundits to declare war on the pro-Palestine socialist group.

That fateful Saturday, the NYC-DSA posted an invitation on X to the Times Square demonstration. It urged people to attend the Sunday demo "in solidarity with the Palestinian people and their right to resist 75 years of occupation and apartheid," then ended with "FREE PALESTINE!" That day's violence against Israeli civilians was not mentioned at all.

On Sunday, October 8, the *New York Post* editorial board issued the first of several bombastic condemnations of the DSA. With uncanny foresight, the tabloid predicted that "Swastikas [would] do the talking" at the Times Square demo plugged by the democratic socialists.

At that afternoon's rally, the mood was jarringly celebratory, especially given the certainty of a massive counterattack by Israel. On the Musk platform, a pro-Israel counter-demonstrator posted a pic of an unidentified young man of color on the pro-Palestine side of the barricades flashing a Nazi symbol on his cellphone.

"Swastika on display as Dem Socialists in NYC declare support for Hamas in terror attack on Israel," blared the cover of the *Post* on Monday, October 9. For the tabloid, it was a conspicuously perfect feedback loop. The fires quickly raged.

"The NYC–DSA's viciousness will spell the end of whatever scant power it has gained in New York City over the past half-decade," declared Nicole Gelinas in the far-right *City Journal*. A columnist for the *Post* (and a frequent contributor to the ideologically indulgent *New York Times*), Gelinas then insisted that "There is no coming back from this."[40]

Eager to expand the circle of attacks, the *Post* soon ran a curious short item about a lesser-known Black minister in Harlem who denounced the DSA. Although several leading figures in the group anchored the pro-Palestine protests, Rev. Johnnie Green criticized only one: Zohran.

Several months before October 7, Mamdani and his DSA allies in the state legislature angered New York powerful pro-Israel networks by introducing the Not on Our Dime act, a measure that would strip the state-approved tax exemption from nonprofits that helped fund Israeli settlements in the West Bank.[41] Zohran also championed BDS.

In the immediate aftermath of October 7, Israel's allies thought they could knock out the DSA. But just over a year and a half later, the group's insurgent candidate crushed the pro-Netanyahu figure backed by most of the New York City elite. Something happened.

*

---

40   Nicole Gelinas, *City Journal* (10-11-2023). The Manhattan Institute, which publishes *City Journal*, is a right-wing think tank that was particularly influential in local politics during the Giuliani administration (1994-2001).
41   In May 2024, AOC announced her support for the legislation, which now included any New York nonprofit that helped subsidize Israel's post-October 7 war crimes in Gaza. The act is still pending in Albany.

Run Zohran Run!

On Tuesday, October 10, the NYC-DSA issued a statement expressing regret over the "timing and tone" of the chapter's since-deleted Saturday tweet. The press release was not at all apologetic about the group's stance towards the larger conflict, however.

"We unequivocally condemn all hatred and the killing of all civilians," read the NYC-DSA's concise statement. The group then forcefully denounced the Netanyahu's "complete siege" of Gaza—which had already cut off electricity, food and water in the occupied territory—as well as the "collective punishment" of civilians for the actions of Hamas. The chapter's two-paragraph statement closed by calling for "the end of U.S. military aid for occupation and apartheid."

The NYC-DSA's "sorry, not sorry" response in no way mollified the group's many foes, nor was it meant to do so. Bronx congressman Ritchie Torres, who became AIPAC's leading New York City social media influencer after October 7, clearly consulted a thesaurus before posting that the activist group's statement was "despicable, detestable, disgraceful and disgraced."

Mayor Eric Adams, whose ties to Turkey's authoritarian Erdoğan regime would eventually lead to federal corruption charges, soon weighed in on Israel's behalf. He told MSNBC host Joe Scarborough, "You had the DSA and others carrying swastikas and calling for the extermination of Jewish people." Shockingly, the mayor's lies went unchallenged.

Zohran was a prominent figure at many of the pro-ceasefire rallies that sprouted up across the city after Israel initiated its collective punishment of Gaza a few days after the Hamas attacks. Along with his DSA colleague Assemblywoman Marcela Mitaynes (who represents Brooklyn's Sunset Park), Zohran joined a large protest organized by Jewish Voice for Peace outside of Chuck Schumer's home on Prospect Park West on Friday night, October 13.

"Tonight we are on the brink of genocide of the Palestinian people," Mamdani told the gathering of over one thousand activists. "Following the horrific murders of Israelis, we are seeing that Israel intends to level Gaza," Zohran stated.

After he and Mitaynes joined scores of activists in getting arrested (for blocking traffic), Zohran was detained for four-and-a-half hours and received two summonses. "I plan to continue to speak out against this impending genocide of Palestinians and use every avenue available to me to make it clear that New Yorkers oppose this indiscriminate killing of civilians," Mamdani stated after his release. Mass slaughter "cannot happen on our watch, and it cannot happen on our dime."[42]

The following Friday night, Mamdani and Mitaynes were joined by a slew of other DSA elected officials at a Manhattan march. Along with leftwing Muslim councilmember Shahana Hanif (who represents Brooklyn's Park Slope, Windsor Terrace and her home turf in Kensington),

---

42 Qns.com (10-14-2023).

Mitaynes, and DSA state senator Jabari Brisport engaged in civil disobedience.

There were no Swastika sightings at either of the two large protests. But that didn't stop Israel hawks from linking the DSA to the Times Square rally and the random teenager who flashed the Nazi symbol in the direction of a militant Zionist.[43]

As seen by the post-October 7 actions of Zohran, his fellow DSA elected officials, and the group's defiant local chapter, when threatened by powerful opponents, the insurgents clearly assumed a far different stance than far larger, more longstanding institutions (e.g. Columbia University). Rather than cave in, Mamdani and his DSA comrades forcefully stood their ground.

One year before he announced his mayoral run, Zohran and company were battle-tested.

---

43 After Zohran's primary win, David G. Greenfield, an Orthodox Jewish nonprofit leader who regularly denounces pro-Palestine protests, revived the spurious DSA-Swastika link on *Inside City Hall* (7-7-2025).

CHAPTER 4
The Message is a Mantra

Eight days after Eric Adams took office on Jan 1, 2022, a massive fire broke out at Twin Parks, a high-rise apartment complex in the central Bronx. One unit's faulty space heater sparked the blaze, and a defective safety door-mechanism allowed it to spread. Seventeen people died (with dozens more seriously injured), many of whom were Muslim immigrants from the West African nation of Gambia.

Mayor Adams responded by advising the city's millions of apartment dwellers to "close the doors" when a fire started, thus ignoring the Twin Parks landlord's neglect. (In general, the use of space heaters suggests that a building's owners are not providing sufficient heat, as required by city law.) Along with housing advocates, the NYC-DSA sharply criticized Adams' response, tweeting that the mayor "blame[d] the victims, not the landlord."

As the same DSA post further noted, the co-founder of Camber Property Group, whose many residential holdings included Twin Parks, was a member of Adams' transition team. Two and a half years later, a press release from the mayor's office quoted the Camber honcho's positive comments about an Adams housing initiative. The self-styled "blue-collar mayor" frequently rolled with the 1%.[44]

This was by no means the first clash between the billionaire-friendly mayor and the DSA. "'Running against a movement': Eric Adams declares war on AOC's socialists," declared a *New York Post* headline in July 2021. At a fundraiser for the general election in upscale Douglaston, a northeast Queens neighborhood near the Nassau County border, the center-right Democratic candidate circled the wagons against what he called the "DSA socialists," a slightly redundant term.

The leftist "movement," declared the self-aggrandizing future mayor, was "mobilizing to stop Eric Adams. They realize that if I'm successful, we're going to start the process of regaining control of our cities." The event was co-hosted by a Republican city councilmember.[45]

---

44 During his late-night hours, the flashy mayor notoriously frequented Zero Bond, a members-only club in Lower Manhattan where Wall Street hot shots and large real estate players cut deals.
45 Adams appointed that ally, Eric Ulrich, as his first commissioner of the city's notoriously corrupt Department of Buildings. In September 2023, Manhattan District Attorney Alvin Bragg indicted Ulrich on sixteen felony counts of bribery, leading to the commissioner's resignation.

During Adams' first year at City Hall, the DSA helped organize protests at public hearings held by the Rent Guidelines Board (RGB), which determines the yearly rates for the city's one million rent-stabilized units. The DSA's two city councilmembers, Alexa Avilés and Tiffany Cabán (both elected in 2021), held town hall meetings and encouraged their supporters to attend the board's hearings that spring.

After the Adams-appointed RGB approved a 3.25% increase in mid-2022, "Eric Adams Raised My Rent" became a DSA rallying cry. Zohran wore a shirt featuring that statement while running the November 2022 NYC Marathon. At a May 2023 RGB hearing, Cabán and three leftist city council allies (Shahana Hanif, Sandy Nurse, and Chi Ossé) stormed the stage to dramatize their objection to the board's hikes.

Outside of a June 2024 Manhattan RGB meeting, Zohran went one step further, joining housing activists in civil disobedience. A photo in *Gothamist* showed the assemblymember in handcuffs, shouting in unison with other demonstrators while surrounded by a phalanx of NYPD officers.

Prior to announcing his run for mayor, over the next few months Zohran met with tenant advocacy groups including CAAAV, which works with Asian communities across the city. Tenants PAC, led by veteran city housing activist Mike McKee, had strongly criticized Adams' pro-landlord RGB since 2022. So did the Community Service Society, one of the city's most longstanding anti-poverty organizations.

Run Zohran Run!

The main item on Zohran's 2025 platform—a call to "freeze the rent" for four years—thus stemmed directly from the activist work by the DSA in conjunction with various grassroots organizations. After three years of supporting his RGB's rent hikes (of 3.25%, 3%, and 2.75%), amid his reelection bid in June 2025 Adams called for the board "to issue the lowest increase possible."

When the RGB determined that there would be another 3% increase, Adams insisted that the board "exercised their independent judgment" and claimed to be "disappointed" by his appointees' decision. Without mentioning Zohran by name, a City Hall press release stated that "While freezing the rent may sound like a catchy slogan, it is bad policy, short-sighted, and only puts tenants in harm's way."

As Zohran highlighted during the primary, an RGB report released in late March showed that between 2022 and 2023 (the most recent year fully calculated), rent-stabilized landlords' profit margin went up by 12%. Adams went to bat for the private equity investors and real estate speculators that own most of the rent-stabilized buildings. Mamdani spoke on behalf of the roughly 2.5 million tenants living inside those apartments.

From day one of his campaign, Mamdani owned the rent freeze issue. The primary results proved it to be a winning position.

*

In his second term in Albany, Mamdani teamed up with State Senator Michael Gianaris, a former Arvella Simotas ally who represents greater Astoria. The two Democrats designed a pilot program for free buses. In a September 2024 joint piece in *The Nation*, the lawmakers explained that two major U.S. cities with progressive mayors—Boston (led by Michelle Wu[46]) and Kansas City (under Quinton Lucas)—had launched similar initiatives. Mamdani and Gianaris called their trial balloon a "resounding success."

That statement was not just two pols tooting their own horns. Starting in the summer of 2023, the New York state legislature funded a one-year experiment that saw one bus line in each borough allow riders to board for free. The MTA reported that the open access resulted in a sizable spike in ridership on each line, with the largest uptick among riders with a yearly income of less than $28,000, for whom the $2.90 cost per ride is an obstacle.

A transit workers union official informed the lawmakers that the "fare box is responsible for 50% of the assaults on my operators. Free bus service would make my bus operators' job much safer." Countless bus riders and drivers thus supported the Mamdani-Gianaris effort.

The Nation byline listed Zohran first, and it's easy to see his influence on both the program and the legislators' recap. "The cost of a ride is just one more example of a cost-of-living crisis," the story noted at the outset, hyperlinking to a United Way report finding that 50% of New York City residents were "struggling to cover their basic needs."

---

[46] Asked at a televised debate in June to name the nation's "most effective Democrat," Mamdani chose Wu (b. 1985).

Unlike Kamala Harris, Chuck Schumer, and Hakeem Jeffries, in the summer and early autumn of 2024, Zohran paid close attention to the struggles faced by countless working-class people. While national Democratic Party leaders insisted that the Biden economy was strong, Mamdani focused on the everyday hardship that the Dem brass did not want to acknowledge.

After Adams' indictment in late September 2024, Mamdani discussed the charges on *Democracy Now!* As Zohran told Amy Goodman, "The same mayor who allegedly received over $100,000 in bribes was just last week praising New York police officers for opening fire on four New Yorkers at a subway station over the crime of stealing a $2.90 subway fare." The prospective mayoral candidate thus connected high-level corruption to policing and inequality, previewing the affordability agenda he would soon roll out.

On October 23, the day he officially joined the race, Zohran told Goodman and co-host Juan Gonzalez that in addition to freezing the rent, "We are going to make buses free and fast across this entire city." In their *Nation* article, Mamdani and Gianaris did not mention the increased speed of buses. But as the DSA candidate would explain many times on the primary trail, bus stops with lines of passengers paying the fare are the biggest reason for delays. As riders smooth out dollar bills and insert coins, the bus falls behind schedule.

As Mamdani told Goodman and Gonzalez, the third main component of his agenda was "universal childcare at no cost for all New Yorkers for children from the ages of six weeks to five years." Public daycare access was an issue central to progressive Maya Wiley's platform in her 2021 run in the Democratic primary for mayor. Wiley, a longtime civil rights activist, had been an official in the de Blasio administration, during which the rollout of universal pre-kindergarten access in the city's public schools saved parents' thousands of dollars in childcare costs for four-year-olds.

In his second term, de Blasio had pushed for kindergarten to include three-year-olds. For unclear reasons, Mayor Adams balked at supporting that expansion until his reelection year. Mamdani's more comprehensive childcare proposal promised to save parents with young children a significant amount of money.

From day one, Zohran's message was clear: *He would fight for an affordable city by freezing the rent, making buses fast and free, and providing universal childcare.* Or simply, *Freeze the rent. Make buses free. Provide childcare.* Along with the candidate, Mamdani's volunteers individually repeated the trio of pledges hundreds of times—and collectively did so in the millions—as they interacted with voters across the five boroughs. The trinity of proposals formed the campaign's mantra.

*

Throughout the primary, the DSA candidate's extensive policy ideas could be found via Zohran for NYC's website. One proposal that he rarely got a chance to discuss in-depth was his call for the creation of a new Department of Community Safety (DCS).

Zohran's plan enables the NYPD to retain its jurisdiction over violent offenses and property crimes. The DCS would address a wide range of antisocial behavioral issues that city residents regularly encounter. Any changes to the criminal justice status quo frightens the city's power elite, however. The *Post*, Cuomo, and other opponents repeatedly attacked Zohran for his past support for "Defund the Police," a call not included in Mamdani's 2025 platform.

As stated on ZohranforNYC.com, the DCS would adopt a "public health approach to safety," focused on mental health intervention teams, including community navigators supervised by licensed medical professionals. It also would contain offices addressing hate crimes and gender-based violence via therapeutic programming. The DCS plan incorporates and expands many proposals advanced by Tiffany Cabán in her 2019 bid for Queens district attorney.

When we spoke in early April, here is how Mamdani explained his rationale for the DCS:

> Our goal is to figure out how we actually deliver public safety. So often, these words are invoked but what is put forward are the same ideas that we've heard for years. There is a reverse New York exceptionalism. We look at things that have worked elsewhere and we say they will never work here because this is New York City and every approach we take must be unique. Rather than genuine exceptionalism, what we often see is mediocrity and failure masquerading as exceptionalism.

According to Alex Vitale, author of the influential work *The End of Policing* (2017), Bill Bratton, NYPD commissioner under both Giuliani and de Blasio, showed no interest in how other cities handled "quality of life" issues. While other police departments applied less punitive strategies, Bratton championed the Broken Windows-based crackdown on all forms of disorder, regardless of the consequences for low-level offenders.

As Vitale explained to the New York City Council's public safety committee this past February, a nearby municipality has already shown that alternatives to traditional policing can be successful. Over the last several years Newark mayor Ras Baraka has initiated community mental health programs similar to those outlined in the DCS plan, leading to dramatic reductions in violent crime in New Jersey's largest city.

"We are looking at cities across the country for public safety initiatives that we can bring to New York City," Zohran told me, rejecting the city's exceptionalism. Vitale notes that in addition to Newark, cities including Baltimore, Minneapolis, Albuquerque, and Los Angeles have offices comparable to the one proposed by Mamdani.

In our conversation, Zohran praised Ras Baraka's forceful opposition to ICE raids in Newark. "I often think of his statement that 'we cannot fight extremism with moderation,'" the candidate noted. In early May, Mamdani joined fellow contender Brad Lander, DSA councilmembers Avilés and Cabán, and comptroller candidate Justin Brannan at a rally denouncing Baraka's arrest by federal agents while he protested outside an ICE detention center in Newark.[47] Meanwhile, Zohran for NYC's platform vowed to end any cooperation between the city and ICE.

*

John Catsimatidis (b. 1948) may not be a household name across the U.S., but he has been a prominent player in New York City politics for several decades. The Greek immigrant is a billionaire, making his fortune first with Manhattan supermarkets while investing in real estate. His portfolio now includes a Brooklyn oil refinery and ownership of WABC radio.

A longtime Republican, Cats (as he refers to himself) is not particularly revered by members of his own party, as illustrated by his loss to Joe Lhota in the 2013 mayoral primary. But the *Post* has him on speed dial, and when the businessman doesn't answer, Murdoch's crew just quotes one of the many hyperbolic assertions the supermarket mogul regularly makes on the *Cats Roundtable*, his Sunday morning radio program aired on the station he owns. NYPD brass enjoy chatting with the big fella.

When Zohran gained steam during the primary, Cats let it be known that he is militantly opposed to Mamdani's plan to open city-run grocery stores in each of the five boroughs. As the insurgent explained on the trail, his assembly district includes the Queensbridge Houses in Long Island City, the largest public housing complex in the U.S. The surrounding area is what advocates call a "food

---

47 On the weekend before the primary, Baraka endorsed Mamdani.

desert," sorely lacking in fresh produce. Supermarkets run by the city would offer all items at cheaper prices, because of reduced rental costs and the elimination of marked-up prices.

"Billionaire John Catsimatidis threatens to close Gristedes chain if socialist Zohran Mamdani is elected NYC mayor," announced a *Post* headline during the last week of the primary. Other Murdoch outlets amplified the declaration. Cats' vow prompted much ridicule on social media, however. Neither Gristedes nor its partner D'Agostino supermarkets are widely revered.

Cats' chains have over two dozen combined stores, almost entirely in Manhattan. All of the locations in their home borough are below 110th Street, where uptown begins and a lot more low-income New Yorkers reside. While the "free market" economy has made him a billionaire, Cats has no business incentive to sell food to working-class people. Mamdani's modest plan would help fill the void.[48]

To a lesser degree than Israel-Palestine, Zohran's public supermarket plan generated disproportionate outrage, stifling the candidate's attempts to call attention to other items on his agenda. An outgrowth of his work for Chhaya, Mamdani advanced several ideas that would help both first-time buyers and long-time homeowners.

---

48 As *Gothamist*'s Ryan Kailath explained in late July, the Economic Development Corporation, a city-owned nonprofit, already runs six markets in four boroughs (not including Staten Island). Zohran did not make that point on the primary trail, however.

Joined by Brooklyn Borough President Antonio Reynoso and local councilmember Chi Ossé, the candidate addressed reporters at Von King Park in Bed-Stuy. Mamdani touted his pledge to create an Office of Deed Theft Prevention, a predatory scheme that has forced many Black homeowners in the area to lose their property and its equity. Only a few reporters attended. But coverage in the *Amsterdam News* informed older Black voters that Zohran was paying attention to their plight.

Like all of his fellow contenders, the Mamdani pledged to build a large amount of new and affordable housing. DSA-aligned housing specialist Cea Weaver helped create a detailed plan. Zohran's proposed number of units—200,000 over ten years—placed him in the more modest range among fellow contenders. Liberal Zellnor Myrie proposed one million (including both new and "preserved" units, a slippery metric) and billionaire Whitney Tilson promised two million.

In mid-April, the frontrunner's housing proposal attracted the most attention to the issue, but the mini-scandal that transpired did not help the former governor. "Andrew Cuomo Used ChatGPT for his Housing Plan," announced a *Hell Gate* headline on Sunday night, April 13. The worker-owned outlet's Max Rivlin-Nadler and Christopher Robbins explained that the first 27 of Cuomo's 29-page document were "fairly unremarkable." But on page 28, things came unglued.

As Max and Chris amusingly detailed, the last two pages were full of typos, gobbledygook, and material generated by ChatGPT, the generative A.I. writing tool. It was not hard for the two reporters to establish that humans did not create the material found on the final pages of Cuomo's plan. The URL link in a footnote ended with the company's name. After the campaign's ornery spokesman Rich Azzopardi first claimed that ChatGPT was simply "a research tool," Cuomo's team later blamed the foolishness on a campaign adviser, identifying that person by name.

Whether sincere or not, no candidate was able to speak in-depth about the city's dire housing shortage. There were too many contenders and the details of how to build affordable units are intricate.

*

In early March, Zohran made a bold move: He sat down for an interview with the *Post*. The insurgent knew he was giving Murdoch's crew something they would denounce. "Socialist NYC mayoral candidate wants to hike corporate taxes to pay for loads of freebies," the ensuing headline declared. Some readers no doubt were aghast. Many others were likely intrigued.

As Mamdani later explained to progressive YouTube host Jack Cocchiarella, "We told the *Post* reporters the same thing we tell everyone else: 'We will tax the most profitable corporations at the same rate as the radical socialist utopia of New Jersey and use those taxes to pay for things that'll improve the lives of every New Yorker.'" Zohran's cheeky reference to the Garden State got plenty of social media attention.

Run Zohran Run!

Zohran also announced that he would raise taxes on New Yorkers with incomes over $1 million per year. As Bloomberg.com reported in July, the latest data (from 2022) shows that the total number of city residents in that category is between 34,000-35,000, a mere fraction of the city's nearly 8.5 million people.[49] Both the *Post* and the *Times* nonetheless ran numerous stories questioning Zohran's harsh treatment of this embattled group.

New York City, however, does not have the ability determine to its own income and corporate tax rates. The state legislature needs to approve such changes, and Gov. Kathy Hochul, a centrist Democrat, assured the business elite that she would veto any tax hikes. As of the end of July, Hochul had not yet endorsed Mamdani.

As the primary race took shape, it was easy for Zohran's fellow contenders and media antagonists to dismiss his promises of free buses, universal childcare, and city-run grocery stores as unrealistic because of their cost.[50] The campaign coincided with the annual budget negotiations at City Hall. For the fiscal year that started this July 1, the city's spending outlay totaled over $115 billion, more than two times greater than the state budget of Illinois, which has four million more residents than New York City. Mamdani also proposed reallocating some of that very large pot to fund his initiatives.

---

49   When calculated by net worth, the number of millionaires surpasses 350,000. Nearly everyone who owns an apartment in Manhattan falls into that category. Zohran's proposal thus targets income.
50   A rent freeze is revenue neutral because the stabilized buildings are privately owned.

In 2013, Bill de Blasio campaigned on a pledge to fund universal pre-k via a tax on the rich. Gov. Andrew Cuomo, a reliable ally of the 1%, responded by moving money around in the state budget in order to finance UPK without tapping elite wallets. As de Blasio noted in June 2025, New York City's upper crust stood to reap hefty dividends from Trump's tax cuts. Meanwhile, the billionaires made a bad bet that Cuomo would win the primary.

At the outset of August, Mamdani clearly had the wind at his back, thus increasing his ability to force Gov. Hochul into supporting tax hikes on the ultra-elite. Hochul is up for reelection in 2026.

*

Before we return to the outset of Zohran's 2025 run, here are a few things to keep in mind:

1. New York City has a very generous campaign finance program that currently provides 8-1 matching funds, setting these ground rules for the mayoral race:

   - $10, the minimum amount that is supplemented, yields $90.
   - $2,100 is the maximum contribution. If a donor lives in the city, $250 becomes $2,250 (making the largest individual donation yield $4,350).
   - A candidate must obtain 1,000 discrete contributions from city residents in order to get the extra funds.
   - The 1,000 donations must total at least $250,000.
   - Donors must list their employers.

- The New York City Campaign Finance Board scrutinizes the contributions.

2. Since 2021, city primaries have followed a ranked-choice voting process, meaning:

    - Voters list their preferred candidates, starting with their first choice (1) through their fifth (5). A ballot with fewer than five selections still counts.
    - Candidates may cross-endorse each other in order to get second-place rankings.
    - Elected officials, unions, advocacy groups and others sometimes propose an initial slate to rank without listing a candidate as number one. Later in the campaign the same endorser may opt to make a candidate their top choice. In the following chapters, I only mention when Zohran became the number-one pick by various political players.

3. A few other points about how the story proceeds.

    - Although I mention several national media outlets' coverage of Mamdani's primary run, which expanded infinitely in June, I devote far more attention to local media. My aim is to capture how New York City voters gathered information about the race. National and international coverage certainly can contribute to local views, but candidates typically need to first gain traction in the five boroughs before they generate significant interest elsewhere.
    - As seen thus far, when I discuss stories from leading outlets including the *Times* and the *Post*, I

frequently do not name the reporters listed on the bylines. I chose not to do so in many cases because a large portion of anti-Zohran stories appeared to be strongly shaped by heavy-handed editors.

Without further ado, off we go...

PART TWO:
ASCENT

CHAPTER 5
Fast Start

In the initial stages of the 2025 Democratic primary, Zohran and fellow candidates believed they would need to topple a hobbled incumbent. The long-swirling rumors that Mayor Eric Adams would face corruption charges became reality in late September 2024, when federal prosecutors announced a five-count indictment accusing the mayor of bribery and campaign finance offenses.

The purported wrongdoing dated back to Adams' tenure as Brooklyn borough president (2014-2021) and continued throughout his first term in City Hall. According to Damian Williams, lead prosecutor for the Southern District of New York (SDNY), Adams had received "illegal benefits" from Turkish officials that resulted in that nation's new high-rise embassy near the UN opening without passing the required fire inspection.

Jocelyn Strauber, Adams' appointee as head of the city's Department of Investigation, fully cooperated with the

SDNY and FBI. "As charged, this illegal conduct compromised [Adams'] integrity as an elected official," Strauber stated. The SDNY indictment marked the first time that a sitting mayor of New York City faced criminal charges. Over forty elected officials—including AOC, Zohran, and fellow DSA elected officials, along with many mainstream Democrats—quickly called for Adams to resign. Several high-ranking members of his administration departed, but Adams stayed in office.

"It is impossible for the mayor to perform his duties," Zohran told *Democracy Now!* host Amy Goodman a few days after the SDNY indictment. "The same mayor who allegedly received over $100,000 in bribes was just last week praising New York police officers for opening fire on four New Yorkers at a subway station over the crime of stealing $2.90 of a subway fare." The prospective candidate had been refining his messaging, connecting every issue to affordability.

When Zohran sat down with *Democracy Now!* co-hosts Goodman and Juan Gonzalez on the day his campaign launched (Wednesday, October 23), all three assumed that defeating Adams remained the goal. Mamdani explained that in his view, the mayor's pledge to focus on the federal charges would short-change "working-class New Yorkers." In the candidate's view, Adams had been "failing" to address the needs of city residents well before the indictment. The "true crisis," Zohran said, was the skyrocketing cost-of-living in the city.

Mamdani vowed that if elected he would impose a rent freeze, expand free bus transportation and enact universal childcare. The then-longshot's message was the same on October 23 as it would be when he unexpectedly won the primary the following June 24. Mamdani further assured Goodman that he was proud to belong to the "democratic socialist tradition."

When Gonzalez noted that Mamdani's position on Palestine was "not normally a plank" for a New York City mayoral candidate "but certainly will affect how people vote," Zohran reiterated his opposition to the "taxpayer-funded genocide." He did not have time to discuss the incumbent's stridently pro-Israel politicking. But most *Democracy Now!* listeners were surely aware that Mayor Adams wholeheartedly backed the NYPD's violent crackdown on pro-Palestine campus protests.

In a *Guardian* story published on October 23, Zohran told reporter Erum Salam that he would target "sets of voters that have been erased" from city politics—adding that some groups "have been persecuted by the political system in the city." Mamdani provided an example from the Astoria assembly district he represents. In the aftermath of 9/11, he noted, Steinway Street was where Mayor Bloomberg "created the demographics unit within the NYPD to illegally surveil Muslims on the basis of our faith. And now the representative of that street is going to run for the same position that created that [unit]." Mamdani's success illustrates how dramatically the city has changed in the past 25 years.

On the same day Zohran announced his run, his campaign posted a cutting-edge 100-second launch video. Wearing a thigh-length white South Asian shirt, Zohran walks down a residential street in Astoria while succinctly describing his main platform planks. Text across the screen introduces the candidate as Zohran Kwame Mamdani.

After highlighting Mayor Adams' corruption charges (and briefly weaving in a shot of then-Governor Cuomo during the pandemic), the up-tempo video mixes action shots of Zohran with statements from everyday New Yorkers describing the hardships they face. A woman wearing a keffiyeh while pushing a stroller states, "I want to raise my kid in New York." Zohran does not mention Palestine, but the scarf speaks loudly.

Zohran scripted the video with campaign manager Elle Bisgaard-Church, media strategist Morris Katz, and communications director Andrew Epstein. It was produced by Fight Agency, a Democratic consulting firm that employs Katz. Shortly after its release, I showed it to a focus group of a dozen undergraduate college students in Brooklyn, most of whom grew up in the city. The response was entirely favorable.

At the evening launch party in Long Island City, Cynthia Nixon lent her star power in support of the candidate she called "a movement person," and a diverse group of activists brought people power. Ashik Siddique, the national DSA's co-chair raised in a Bangladeshi Muslim household in Brooklyn, observed that "everybody I've talked to in the past few days is so hype for this."

Jaslin Kaur, a Sikh Punjabi activist who—running as a DSA candidate—lost a close Democratic primary race for city council in 2021 in the central Queens neighborhood in which she grew up, shared Siddique's enthusiasm. "I really don't want to get priced out of the city I love," said Kaur, "and I'm so excited that a South Asian, Muslim candidate is stepping up." Brooklynite Asad Dandia, a Muslim raised in a Pakistani American household in Brighton Beach, explained that he supported Zohran because "I'm simply tired that my rent is going up."

The campaign's Instagram recap included a twenty-something woman wearing a hijab stating that Zohran "is one of the only politicians who has stood up for Palestine." On a lighter note, one lad claims that he supports the DSA candidate because a halal plate of chicken with rice used to cost three dollars and now it's ten bucks—what the candidate would soon refer to as "halal-flation." "What the fuck?" asks the young brown man, who is wearing a Rosa Parks t-shirt.

Eight months later, many of the same opening-night attendees returned to Long Island City for an even bigger Zohran event.

*

Two days before the 2024 election, Zohran ran his second New York City marathon. In his first, in 2022, the DSA assemblymember wore a shirt reading, "Eric Adams Raised My Rent!" Two years later, the back of his jersey vowed, "Zohran Will Freeze It!"

Although he improved by 25 minutes over his performance two years earlier, Mamdani's 2024 marathon time of nearly five hours and 40 minutes meant that he finished the race in a rather distant 48,013th place. Nonetheless, "I'm outpacing all the mayoral contenders in the race," Zohran quipped along the route to reporter Jeff Coltin, of *Politico*'s New York Playbook.

In the *Democracy Now!* launch-day interview with Zohran, Juan Gonzalez mentioned the ongoing speculation that Andrew Cuomo would join the crowded field. But Mamdani instead focused on the Adams administration's inattention to the city's housing crisis. The former governor's candidacy did not become official until early March.

In the meantime, Adams further angered New York Democrats by cozying up to the White House. In the wake of his September 2024 indictment, the mayor started making overtures to Trump, repeatedly asserting (without evidence) that the DoJ's corruption charges resulted from his outspoken criticism of the Biden administration's immigration policies.

Although he endorsed Kamala Harris, Adams did not campaign for her. Nor did he criticize Trump as election day neared. At his late October rally at Madison Square Garden, Trump declared that Adams had been "treated very badly" because of the mayor's stance on immigration.

After Trump's share of the vote in New York City spiked from 23% in 2020 to 31% in 2024, some analysts called it a "red wave."[51] Political observers now questioned whether

---

51 The real story was the drop-off in Democratic turnout from Biden in 2020. Over 400,000 Biden voters did not cast ballots for Harris. Trump collected roughly 150,000 more tallies than four years earlier.

Adams, a Republican in the 1990s, might switch parties again and run as the MAGA candidate for mayor.

Trump's November 2024 victory also led to the first time Zohran's mayoral campaign caught fire on social media. Rather than question why some working-class voters now backed Trump or simply did not turn out for Harris from his armchair, the candidate hit the streets and asked many people directly.

Zohran chose two locations—Hillside Avenue in Jamaica, Queens, and Fordham Road in the central Bronx—that witnessed shifts towards the right in the last two presidential elections. A strikingly diverse range of working-class residents told Mamdani that they voted for Trump.

"They liked Trump because they don't want the Palestinian brothers killed," a middle-aged pharmacist observes regarding residents of Jamaica, a neighborhood known as "Little Bangladesh." A Black respondent in his thirties, a middle-aged South Asian man, and an elderly Latina explain that Trump may bring back "lower prices" for groceries.

As two Black women under forty tell Zohran, Palestine was the main reason many people they knew did not turn out for Harris. They and others fault the Democrats' neglect of pocketbook issues. Several people respond enthusiastically to Mamdani's bread-and-butter platform.

Over the next six months, Mamdani's tweet featuring the three-minute video would be viewed over 2.5 million times. The immediate splash after the post went up in mid-November caught the attention of media observers not aligned with mainstream Democrats.

"This is so good," tweeted Briahna Joy Gray, national press secretary for the 2020 Bernie Sanders campaign. In late November, former **MSNBC** host Mehdi Hasan led off his interview with Mamdani on *Zeteo*—a news site Hasan founded in 2024—by showing clips of Zohran's Trumpers-on-the-streets interviews. The host asked Mamdani whether Trump's gains in the city reflected a shift in the electorate away from a working-class agenda.

"Many politicians across New York City and New York State are using this as an opportunity to air their previously held positions about whether the left should be part of a governing coalition," Zohran observed. "But when I went out and spoke to New Yorkers directly, I found that their economic concerns are what's at the heart of a left economic program."

Although Trump's campaign pledges were "insincere and ridiculous," Zohran observed, the salesman-president at least offered voters "a promise" that prices of household goods would return to their pre-pandemic levels. Meanwhile, the Harris campaign paid scant attention to voters' struggles to pay their bills.

*

Mamdani created another social media sensation on New Year's Day. This time the splash was literal, with Zohran dipping into the ice-cold water at Coney Island as part of the Polar Bear Club's annual January 1 plunge.

As reporter Haidee Chu recounted in *The City*, a local nonprofit newsroom, the candidate was sporting a dark grey suit he had purchased a suit for $30 at an Astoria thrift store. Zohran declared that he was "freezing your rent as the next mayor of New York City. Let's plunge into the details." He then did a running head-first dive into Lower New York Bay.

While locals of various ages and shapes frolicked in the water, Mamdani gleefully launches into a spiel about his rent freeze plan. Few fellow plungers appear to be thinking about the Rent Guidelines Board, but while toweling off, Zohran succinctly explains how Eric Adams' appointees had consistently raised rents during the mayor's first three years in office. He then quotes the landlord-mayor's absurdist assertion that "I am real estate."[52]

At once madcap and wonky, Mamdani's Coney Island video racked up over 800,000 views across various platforms by the time Chu's article came out three weeks later. "Humor often is far more effective at having someone open up to even consider you," the candidate observed.

As Andrew Epstein notes, it was Mamdani's idea to attend the New Year's Day event, and only the two of them went. After his dip, Zohran held their stuff while Andrew dived in, with the longshot mayoral contender shivering on the

---

52 Adams' four-unit building in Bed-Stuy does not qualify for rent stabilization, which requires six or more units. In the homestretch of the 2021 primary, Adams faced swirling questions about whether he lived in the basement apartment of his building. Most observers believed he resided in Fort Lee, New Jersey (just across the George Washington Bridge).

beach in a very wet suit. He would not be standing alone for long in 2025.

The plunge was just one of several videos posted by Zohran on social media that had recently caught fire. In addition to the Trump voter conversations, Chu cited his amusing skit with Brooklyn comedian Cassie Wilson, in which the latter plays the role of the "naysayer." Mamdani also "intervened" in a satirical diner debate about between two older white New Yorkers, one who claims to like Adams while the other supports Cuomo.

Less-scripted postings that captured eyeballs featured the DSA candidate asking city food truck vendors about what Zohran dubbed "halal-flation," referring to rising prices at food trucks. By the middle of January, Zohran's top-flight social media game had put him on the mayoral map.

*

In early January, Zohran bounced across the city to various fundraisers timed to coincide with a Campaign Finance Board deadline.

In order to receive New York City's 8-1 matching funds, a mayoral candidate in the 2025 cycle needed to obtain a minimum of 1,000 donations from city residents, totaling at least $250,000. The filing deadline in order to receive the first 8-1 disbursements was Saturday, January 11, at 11:59 p.m.

While Zohran hopped around to various events, Andrew reached out to early donors, seeking volunteers to appear in a campaign video. Prior to receiving matching funds, Zohran for NYC was a scrappy, low-budget operation.

But the public finance system provided plenty of incentive. Candidates without existing funding networks need to attract as many donors as possible, and social media attention often yields dividends.

In mid-December, a jewelry designer in Staten Island contributed $50 to the campaign (which matching funds would turn into $450). In response to Andrew's inquiry, Jasmine and her husband Matt, a higher-ed administrator, invited Zohran to their home.

A few days later, the candidate visited the couple and their two grade-school age children at their place near the Ferry Terminal, the section of Staten Island that typically votes for Democrats. Zohran, Andrew and a two-person video crew spent 45 minutes or so there. The children took a liking to their friendly guests.

As Mamdani and his team were leaving, Jasmine and Matt's inspired seven-year-old son gave the candidate a Lego creation he made. It was of a mayor wearing a top hat. The boy had high hopes, and Zohran posted the gift on Instagram. The Staten Island home visit formed the basis of a video distributed by the campaign in mid-January.

Fueled by the DSA and other activist networks, Mamdani far exceeded the minimum number of required donors. On Friday, January 10 and the following day, over 1,800 people contributed to the campaign, mostly in the $25-50 range. Because the program requires donors to list their occupations, we know that scores of educators like Matt and numerous creative professionals like Jasmine were excited about Zohran.

Mamdani's first report to the Campaign Finance Board covered the period since he launched his campaign in the fall. He recorded nearly 8,300 donations that totaled over $640,000, crushing the numbers put up by the rest of the mayoral candidates then in the race.[53]

Zohran's January 11 fundraising tour brought him to Sunset Stoop, a recently opened bar and small performance space in Brooklyn's Sunset Park, home to a mix of working-class Latinos and Asians as well as middle-class white homeowners and renters. Since 2020, the area has elected two DSA members, Assemblywoman Marcela Mitaynes and City Councilwoman Alexa Avilés. The warm-up performers that night included a Coney Island sword-swallower.

When Mamdani, sporting a white kurta, took the stage, the candidate joked that upon arriving in the neighborhood, he was confused because he thought the event was actually taking place on someone's front stoop. The mostly 30-something crowd consisted of DSA activists, criminal justice reformers, and educators. After Zohran's brief stump speech, the friendly figure mingled with supporters.

The socialist candidate came to Sunset Park that Saturday evening from an earlier fundraiser in nearby Park Slope. The public transportation candidate assured me that he indeed had taken the B63 bus that connects the two neighborhoods.

---

53   In the three days before the January 11 deadline, Zohran took in $115,000. That included just one maximum contribution of $2,100 (from a Brooklyn physician) and a few others for $1,000. The remainder were less than four figures.

After departing Sunset Stoop, Zohran marched off to Manhattan for another event. As the fast-rising contender told *Hell Gate's* Christopher Robbins a few days later, "I got on [the subway] on Saturday night to go from my second fundraiser to my third fundraiser, and a woman yelled across the platform, 'I just donated to you!'"

As Mamdani explained to Robbins, the campaign's palpable success "is far bigger than any one person. It's about a deep desire to have the city that we all love be one that is affordable for working-class New Yorkers." While bouncing across the five boroughs, Zohran stayed on message.

*

Throughout the winter, Mamdani and his fellow candidates continued to pitch themselves as alternatives to Mayor Adams. The mayor's political future, however, remained in limbo because his federal criminal trial was scheduled for late April, two months before the June 24 primary.

But on Monday, February 10, Emil Bove, then the top deputy attorney general at the Department of Justice, told SDNY prosecutors they should drop the charges against Adams. Danielle Sassoon, the SDNY's lead attorney handling the prosecution, fought to preserve the case. Rather than drop the charges, Sassoon and others on her team resigned.

Amid the fireworks, Trump's extreme-right border czar sat down for a morning interview with Mayor Adams on *Fox & Friends*. With Midtown Manhattan as the backdrop, the crusty border czar and flashy mayor yucked it up while sitting next to each other on the couch. Even though

Bove had explicitly stated that the criminal case hindered Adams' ability to assist with ICE arrests, the mayor insisted that he had not offered anything to the White House in exchange for the dropped charges. Tom Homan quickly undercut Adams' claim.

"I came to New York City and I wasn't going to leave with nothing," Trump's deputy told the hosts. Homan explained that the mayor had indeed agreed to remove the restrictions on ICE access to Rikers Island imposed by the city council during the de Blasio administration. Homan crassly assured the Fox team that if Adams did not follow through on the agreement, he would "come back to New York City, but we won't be sitting on the couch. We'll be in his office, and I will be up his butt saying, 'Where the hell is the agreement we came to?'" Adams smiled nervously.

Many city Democrats were appalled by Adams' craven response to Homan that Friday morning. The cringeworthy exchange made national headlines. "Trump's Border Czar Tells NYC Mayor He'll be 'Up His Butt' if He Breaks Vow to Help ICE," announced NBC News. The following Monday, three prominent deputy mayors (Maria Torres-Springer, Anne Williams-Isom, and Meera Joshi) announced their resignations.

Although Adams would not announce his decision to bow out of the Democratic primary for another six weeks, the handwriting was clearly on the wall. Zohran and his fellow mayoral contenders needed to revise their game plans.

Somewhere in the suburbs, Andrew Cuomo plotted his next move.

CHAPTER 6

A Spicy Mix

"DSA eyes Israel foe for mayor," read a headline of a short news item on page 13 of the *New York Post* on Saturday, October 12, 2024. That Murdoch's minions were eager to restart their year-old battle against the socialist group was no surprise. But how veteran *Post* reporter Carl Campanile ended up with a DSA internal planning document is a head-scratcher.

The NYC-DSA's nomination process nonetheless matched Campanile's description. On Oct. 5, Zohran—labeled by the *Post* as an "Israel-bashing Queens assemblyman"—spoke to the organization's Citywide Electoral Working Group. Along with seven branches within the local chapter, DSA delegates, including the group's elected officials, voted over the next week.

As Campanile reported on October 20, Zohran captured 60% support from the branches and from 107 of 130 delegates. *Jacobin*'s Liza Featherstone explained at the time that dissenters within the ranks questioned Mamdani's electability, fearing that a big loss might weaken the group's various legislative initiatives. But as Zohran told Liza, he "wouldn't run" without the DSA's support.

Having unseated a Democratic Party incumbent in 2020, Zohran was a fast-rising figure among the growing left-wing organization both at the local and national level. In August 2023, Mamdani gave the keynote address at the national DSA convention in Chicago. Now he was the NYC-DSA's first candidate in a citywide race.

Given the outcome of the 2025 primary, it may be surprising that the city's DSA chapter only had approximately 6,600 active members in October 2024. As Zohran's campaign gained steam over the next eight months, the group's ranks grew to 8,800. After Mamdani's resounding triumph over Cuomo, the number quickly surpassed 10,000. Shortly after the primary, the victorious candidate sent out a recruiting statement inviting his legions of fans to join the socialist group.[54]

While the DSA anchored Zohran's dynamic field operation, members of many other activist groups made important contributions. In the summer and early fall of 2024, Zohran met with numerous leaders and organizations to solicit advice and present his vision. As the campaign

---

54 Distributed as a NYC-DSA email blast, Zohran explained his work as a foreclosure counselor and slammed Wall Street for "preying upon" working people. "When the odds are stacked against working people," he said, "the only lasting solution is to come together and create a force big enough to deliver meaningful change."

launched, the grassroots organizations Jewish Voice for Peace (JVP), NY Communities for Change (NYCC), CAAAV, and DRUM Beats declared their support for Zohran.

From day one, Zohran's initial coalition consisted of pro-Palestine activists (JVP and DSA), anti-poverty organizers (NYCC, CAAAV, DRUM, DSA), and East Asian tenants (CAAAV), along with South Asian and Indo-Caribbean city residents (DRUM, CAAAV). Tens of thousands of campaign volunteers, largely from Queens and Brooklyn, shared an affinity with one or more of these viewpoints.

Mamdani's platform resonated with working-class voters across the five boroughs. As his primary campaign gathered steam, NYCC helped Zohran gain traction in the city's Black and Spanish-speaking communities. Mamdani's multicultural legions of foot soldiers were instrumental in making people aware of what the DSA candidate offered.

*

Northwest Queens has been NYC-DSA turf ever since AOC and Cabán's campaigns. Activists view the heavily East Asian neighborhoods around Flushing in northeast Queens as most dominated by Rep. Grace Meng, a moderate Democrat, but liberal State Senator John Liu also wields influence. Southeast Queens, which has a large Black population, continues to be the base for Rep. Greg Meeks, a centrist Democrat.

Although he is Joe Crowley's successor as the Queens Democratic leader, Meeks (b. 1953) by no means influences most political activity across the borough. The tri-partite power structure leaves large swaths of turf in central Queens unclaimed—including fast-growing South Asian neighborhoods bordering Meeks' terrain. Richmond Hill, for example, is home to "Little Guyana." And in November 2024, Zohran conducted post-election interviews with Trump voters in "Little Bangladesh," which runs along Hillside Avenue in northern Jamaica.

Jagpreet Singh is the political director of DRUM Beats, an offshoot of Desis Rise Up & Moving, a nonprofit promoting economic empowerment for South Asian and Indo-Caribbean communities. "Desis" is a Sanskrit term (meaning "country") that diasporic South Asians call themselves, but according to Jagpreet, it's not used by Guyanese, Trinidadian, or other Indo-Caribbeans. As Singh told me, the M.O. of mainstream Democratic leaders in Queens involves sending liaisons to chat up community leaders at various meetings and events. The organizer first worked with the future mayoral candidate at Chhaya from 2018 to 2020. Even prior to Zohran's official campaign launch, Jagpreet said that his role was to introduce Mamdani to many of the same community leaders that the party machine interacts with.

During the early fall 2024, Zohran and Jagpreet, a Sikh Punjabi, attended the Durga Puja festival at a Nepali Hindu temple in Ridgewood, Queens. Just after the campaign launched, the duo appeared at the large Diwali celebration held every fall by Hindus in Richmond Hill's Little Guyana. Two months before the primary, they traveled across the East River to the Sikh Day Parade in Manhattan.

Jagpreet noted that he and Zohran went to countless Bangladeshi events in neighborhoods from City Line in Brooklyn (at the border of Queens) through Hillside Avenue to Parkchester in the east Bronx. As primary day neared, twenty-something Aaron Narraph, one of the DSA's most prominent social media influencers, posted a pic of his Bangladeshi parents expressing support for Zohran.

On Sunday, June 22, Zohran attended a rally in Kensington, Brooklyn with leftist Councilwoman Shahana Hanif, a Bangladeshi Muslim targeted by Israel hawks. Bangladeshi voters helped Hanif crush her challenger, and across the city they helped Mamdani dethrone Cuomo.

*

When Mamdani's campaign launched, CAAAV's political arm announced that the group's "working class Asian immigrant and tenant members" backed Zohran primarily because of his rent freeze position. "We have seen what happens when electeds like Eric Adams take real estate money—year after year, rents go up while New Yorkers work longer for less," stated Alina Shen, organizing director for CAAAV Voice.

CAAAV formed two decades ago as advocacy group for tenants in Manhattan's flagship Chinatown. During the Mamdani campaign Shen led volunteer teams in Brooklyn's Chinatown, which now extends from Sunset Park into Bensonhurst. CAAAV also has a chapter in Astoria that works primarily with Bangladeshi renters.

Run Zohran Run!

On a brisk Sunday in early April, Zohran came to Sunset Park for a "freeze the rent" rally hosted by CAAAV Voice (CV). Brooklyn's large Chinatown starts near the actual park, bringing many older residents to the event, with CV organizers providing Cantonese and Mandarin translation. Plenty of younger Asian activists were also in the mix.

Zohran joined Shen and his fellow DSA figureheads Alexa Avilés and Marcela Mitaynes at the event. When his turn at the mic came, the candidate led the mostly Asian, Spanish-speaking and middle-class white gathering in a call-and-response refrain, with Mamdani belting out "freeze the–" and the crowd yelling "–rent!"

Beside me in the crowd stood two teens, both wearing CAAAV shirts. As Zohran spoke, one said repeatedly to the other, "He's so cool." The sentiment was shared by all ages in attendance.

Two days before the June primary, CV troops would return to Sunset Park to do a final door-knocking push, joining a pre-canvass rally hosted by Jewish Voice for Peace.

*

Zohran's massive, unprecedented ground game was run by the DSA's Tascha Van Auken, who started working in electoral politics in the 2008 Obama campaign. She later managed the successful runs of democratic socialist Julia Salazar in 2018 and Phara Souffrant Forrest two years later.

Helmed by field director Van Auken, Zohran for NYC's outreach operation was nothing if not culturally conversant. Multilingual volunteers spoke to voters in dozens of native languages, from Arabic to Vietnamese. They also distributed informational materials translated into several languages, and the campaign created videos in Urdu, Bangla, and Spanish.

As Van Auken detailed to DSA members in post-primary Zoom call (with over 600 attendees tuning in), by the end of June 24, Zohran's campaign had 30,000 active volunteers and 20,000 additional participants. Nearly 500 trained field leaders directed more than 3,000 canvasses in over 60 neighborhoods across the five boroughs.

One month before the primary, Zohran's team predicted that the campaign's volunteers would knock on over one million voter doors. By the end of June 24, Van Auken reported, the tally reached a whopping 1.6 million. Participants made over 2.3 million calls. During the homestretch, voters heard from prominent voices including Naomi Klein, who headlined a phone bank event.

All who participated in voter outreach, Van Auken observed, felt the sensation of "collective power" to varying degrees. That muscle memory, she forecasted, will contribute to innumerable future campaigns, regardless of whether they are led by the DSA.

On the afternoon of June 23, yours truly was at home in Sunset Park chatting about the book you're reading with OR publisher Colin Robinson. During our call my doorbell rang. Sure enough, it was a canvasser for Mamdani and Avilés visiting my apartment building, for at least the fourth time that primary season.

Run Zohran Run!

At a televised debate in June, a very rich but politically impoverished mayoral candidate ludicrously claimed that Zohran's momentum resulted simply from "cute videos." Some candidates needed to get out more.

*

"It's not just white kids," Iggy Sanchez said about his fellow Mamdani volunteers. Sanchez is a twenty-something raised in the Bronx now living in Brooklyn. "It's not just transplants," Iggy states. "It's moms. It's immigrants. It's just people who want a slightly more affordable city. That really moved me."

Sanchez's account is one of several post-primary reflections compiled by *Indypendent* publisher John Tarleton. Twenty-something Amanda Vender explains how she gained access to large apartment buildings in Northwest Queens: "When I had to choose which buzzer to ring first to enter a building, I consulted the MiniVAN app[55] on my phone and always went with a voter under 35 because I knew they'd be a likely [Mamdani] supporter and let me in."

"At one door in Sunnyside," recounts Vender, "two children around 6 and 8 years old answered the door. I introduced myself and asked for the parents. 'Our parents aren't home,' one said, 'but we want our parents to vote for Zohran!'"

---

55 MiniVAN is a database of Democratic voters used by many campaigns.

Jose Sanchez (who is not related to Iggy) is in his early thirties and identifies as a gay Afro-Puerto Rican. Jose told John that he first participated in politics when he took the train from his home in New Jersey to join Occupy Wall Street. The Occupy practice of mutual aid surfaced during Jose's voter outreach for Zohran. On the sweltering hot primary day, a woman at poll site in Crown Heights saw that Sanchez was drenched in sweat and poured water from her bottle into Jose's.

A veteran organizer with NYCC, Pete Sikora won over many of his neighbors in Brooklyn's Carroll Gardens, an upscale progressive area that Brad Lander formerly represented in the City Council. Pete said that he regularly sat on his front stoop for "an hour or three" persuading Lander supporters to back Mamdani. He "met a lot of neighbors" and someone even left a note on his building's door thanking Pete for his advice. "Don't ever let anyone tell you otherwise," Sikora told Tarleton. "One-to-one contact works!"

In the wake of Zohran for NYC's resounding grassroots victory, many future Democratic campaigns in the city and elsewhere surely will expand their direct outreach to voters. But Mamdani did not inspire thousands of volunteers to devote their leisure time to his campaign because he has some sort of guru-like appeal. "Zohran's message is really what set him apart," Ozone Park canvass leader Felicia Singh (no relation to Jagpreet) told me.

The campaign featured Mamdani's cost-of-living agenda on buttons with simple phrases like "Freeze the Rent," "Fast, Free Busses" and "Universal Childcare." Enthusiastic volunteers sporting those badges chatted with voters and handed them vibrant campaign materials that featured the same proposals.

Meanwhile, none of the other mayor candidates in the primary offered signature policy ideas that were easy to deliver. For example, Brad Lander's main plan was to convert city-owned golf courses into residential housing, a complex process that would take several years. Many voters had more immediate concerns.

Zohran rolled out his crystal-clear affordability agenda on day one, his volunteer army brought it to front doors across the five boroughs, and voters gave them a very friendly reception.

*

In addition to the campaign's ground game, Zohran's skillful use of social media helped him move into second place by early April. He was already well-known in both activist circles and among the city's South Asian communities, dating back to his advocacy for taxi drivers. Zohran was now about to become a celebrity in the eyes of young Muslims everywhere.

After the CAAAV rally in Sunset Park, Zohran and Andrew Epstein headed back to Astoria for an evening with Hasan Piker, a millennial media superstar with a massive fanbase among zoomers. On Twitch, a platform favored by teens, Piker has over 2.7 million followers, with roughly half that number of devotees on TikTok. On YouTube, which spans generations, he has over 1.4 million subscribers.

Hasan is a Turkish American Muslim from New Jersey who, like Zohran, was born in 1991. A *New York Times* style reporter recently characterized Piker's appeal as twofold. There is a "bro" dimension, as the story described: "He likes weapons, inhales supplements, uses nicotine pouches and ruminates endlessly on the legacy of LeBron James." "But unlike many of his contemporaries," the *Times* continued, "Mr. Piker [is] an avowed socialist."

Hasan and Zohran spoke for about an hour, a YouTube-friendly format that allows Piker's team to post clips across platforms. The conversation was far more in-depth than that found in many traditional media outlet interviews with Zohran. They started with his platform but the host then asked the DSA candidate about the MTA, the NYPD, and Rikers Island, with Zohran stating that he would follow through on the city's planned closure of the notorious hellhole.

Although they did not discuss Gaza in much depth, in its rampage against Mamdani the *New York Post* often linked him to Piker, who they referred to as a "sick online influencer" because he frequently criticizes Israel. Without any evidence, the tabloid declared that Hasan was pro-Hamas, thus smearing Zohran as guilty by association.

After the conversation, Piker's Twitch livestream followed the media superstar and the ascending city leader as they went out for a Bangladeshi meal in Astoria. As they walked the streets, numerous young South Asian fans of both figures shook their hands and asked for photos. Many Desis and most young Muslims do not live in the *Post*'s world.

*

Run Zohran Run!

By early June, Zohran was lighting up the city. But it wasn't just young South Asians, DSA members, and pro-Palestine activists who created the buzz. A backyard gathering brought together a range of older fellow travelers. The neighborhood was Brooklyn's historic Fort Greene.

Poet Ken Chen (in his mid-forties) and editor Andy Hsiao (in his early sixties) invited a wide assortment of literati and activists to the latter's house, including many leading figures in New York's Asian community. CNN host W. Kamau Bell joined fellow comedian Hari Kondabolu, a longtime friend of Zohran. *Guardian* columnist Moustafa Bayoumi, a leading Muslim commentator, mingled with Moroccan poet Omar Berrada.

It was not Zohran's short remarks that stood out. Instead, it was the depth of his answers to questions. Joyce Yu, a Chinatown fixture in her seventies, asked the candidate how he would manage the city's Department of Education, which has an annual budget of over $40 billion. She expected the usual "platitudes" about "the importance of a good education," etc. Instead, Yu explained, she was "stunned" by the depth of Zohran's response. He went "line by line" in describing problems in the budget. "He demonstrated knowledge of the challenges of reining in corruption" and discussed how he would work constructively with the powerful teachers union. "He got my vote!" Yu told me.

On that pleasant early June evening in Fort Greene, it was clear to all that the kid had chops. But most dynasties do not end quietly. Over in Midtown East, Goliath revved up his engine.

CHAPTER 7
Dodge Charger

After Andrew Cuomo resigned as governor amid a sexual harassment scandal in August 2021, a simple question lingered: Where did he live?

While in the governor's office for the past decade, Cuomo resided at either the Executive Mansion in Albany or with Sandra Lee, a one-time TV star and Cuomo's second long-time partner, at the large Westchester County home she owned in tawny Mount Kisco, 40 miles north of New York City. The pair split up in 2019.

After Cuomo's resignation in August 2021, where he lived through March 2025 remained a mystery. He did store his stuff at the Westchester mansion owned by his sister Maria and her husband Kenneth Cole, the fashion industry titan. But despite a $250,000 salary and a $5 million book deal, Cuomo had not purchased any property, a curious move for a former Housing and Urban Development (HUD) secretary. In the fall of 2024, as talk of his mayoral run heated up, reporters learned that Cuomo had recently registered to vote from a luxury Midtown building overlooking the East River. One of his daughters, Cara Kennedy-Cuomo,[56] inhabited the swanky unit, which rented for an eye-popping $8,000 per month.

In November 2024, *Hell Gate*'s Adlan Jackson toured Cuomo's new Sutton Place digs, a 38-story tower called "The Oriana." The amply staffed building featured amenities including a cardio gym on the roof deck. "Sutton Place," Jackson observed, "is the New York everyone wants—that's only real in campaign ads and in bygone visions of the city. It makes sense that Cuomo would want to live here if he's revving up a mayoral campaign." By the following March, the former governor had fully moved in, sending Cara to Brooklyn.

Cuomo officially threw his hat into the ring on Saturday, March 1, setting the tone for his primary campaign by releasing a 20-minute video. Unlike Zohran's dynamic 100-second opening ad, the instant-frontrunner's rollout statement was poorly produced and comically dull. Although watching someone speak directly into a camera for 17.5 minutes is generally less than tantalizing, the protracted announcement got plenty of traction on Facebook, the Baby Boomer-preferred site where Cuomo has over 300,000 followers. The instant-frontrunner's large fan club no doubt grew exponentially over the pandemic, when the then-governor delivered

---

56 From 1990-2005, Cuomo was married to Kerry Kennedy, RFK's daughter. The pair had three daughters. The divorce was notoriously acrimonious.

life-or-death information. Zohran's numbers on Facebook lagged behind, at just over 120,000 followers, whereas his next-gen campaign is far more active on Instagram, TikTok and X.

"Intellectually, I have mastered social media," Cuomo informed his favorite reporter, WCBS-TV's Marcia Kramer, two days before the primary. "Practically, I have not mastered it." While the first assertion requires more evidence, the second one was abundantly clear vis-à-vis his announcement video.

A few weeks after Cuomo's launch, Zohran held a presser outside of the Oriana, introducing himself to the former governor's fellow residents. Andrew Epstein had proposed doing the event in order to "disrupt the Rose Garden," referring to the frontrunner's already-evident plan to steer clear of both the public and the press.

Although the Sutton Place appearance captured only modest media attention, it showed that Zohran was unafraid to challenge Goliath on his purported home turf. The insurgent candidate soon began to regularly question the former governor's bona fides as a city dweller, urging his supporters to help "send Andrew Cuomo back to the suburbs," an effective line of attack that helped undercut frontrunner Andrew Yang four years earlier.[57]

It would be erroneous to suggest that Cuomo's time in Westchester or Albany meant that he was unaware

---

57   During the pandemic Yang lived in New Paltz, 80 miles north of New York City.

of what was happening in New York City. But the lens through which he viewed the sprawling metropolis was quite narrow. During the nearly fifteen years he spent as a statewide elected official, Cuomo presided over two large Manhattan offices. The attorney general often works from an outpost in the financial district, whereas the governor is frequently at 3rd Avenue near 41st Street, close to Grand Central Station.

When the primary entered the homestretch in June, the *New York Times* asked Cuomo when he last lived in New York City. The answer? The late 1980s.

*

A charmless, high-rise center of power, Midtown East suited the most recent Governor Cuomo, who cut deals with many Manhattan real estate titans from there. Until his first term in office, Donald Trump regularly resided at a nearby place from which he famously launched his initial presidential campaign.

The developer built Trump Tower (at 5th Avenue between 56th and 57th Street) in the early 1980s with plenty of assistance from Mayor Ed Koch. Two decades later, like most large players in New York City real estate, Trump helped fill Cuomo's coffers.

As Cynthia Nixon highlighted in her 2018 run against Cuomo, between 2001 and 2009 the developer's ante to Andrew was $64,000. Like most politicians, Cuomo indignantly asserted that the money did not influence his actions. "I am going to be deeply critical of [Trump] and keep the contributions," the governor declared, in response to Nixon.

The future president viewed his transactions with politicians differently. "When you give [money to pols], they do whatever the hell you want them to do," Trump observed in 2016.[58]

During Cuomo's reign as governor, New York State's campaign finance system remained far less progressive than New York City's. Sky-high limits on contributions enabled Trump's fellow real estate titans to drop large sums in the multiple campaign accounts controlled by Cuomo.

Between 2010 and 2018, Len Blavatnik, a business associate of Trump's 2016 campaign manager Paul Manafort, deposited over $350,000 into the governor's war chest. In 2013, a leading developer of "Supertall" luxury towers near Central Park gave Cuomo $100,000 (and the state Democratic Party account another $100,000), yielding legislation that provided favorable tax breaks.[59]

Trump (b. 1946) and Cuomo (b. 1957) may belong to different political parties, but the two Baby Boomers share plenty of attributes. Both were raised in upscale neighborhoods in eastern Queens, near the border of Long Island's Nassau County. Nepotism indelibly influenced their career paths. Trump inherited his father's real estate empire. Mario Cuomo's son extended a political legacy. Both

---

58 *Washington Post* (9-7-2016).
59 *NY Daily News* (8-9-2013).

Donald and Andrew are bullies who have faced frequent accusations of sexual misconduct.

Just before the June 2025 primary, Marcia Kramer asked the mayoral frontrunner to explain his common roots with the president. "I'm no one to be trifled with," Cuomo replied. "And Trump is no one to be trifled with." After Zohran toppled Cuomo, Trump praised his fellow Boomer, illustrating that the Queens dudes still got along fine.

In 1977, Andrew, then nineteen, cut his teeth in city politics while working on his father Mario Cuomo's dogged, but unsuccessful campaign for mayor. Seeking the law-and-order vote in response to widespread looting that summer, Democrat Ed Koch shamelessly called for the reinstatement of the death penalty, which the legislature had eliminated twelve years earlier. Mario, en route to becoming a leading Catholic politician of the late twentieth century (alongside his friend Joe Biden), remained a steadfast opponent of capital punishment. After losing to Koch in the mayoral primary, the elder Cuomo opted to run as the Liberal Party candidate in the general election. Koch won easily.

It was during their next showdown with Koch that the Cuomo duo began to forge deep alliances with Black leaders and voters across the city. After the 1977 primary, Harlem's influential Congressman Charles Rangel had endorsed Koch. During his first term, Koch angered many Black leaders, causing Rangel to back Cuomo in the 1982 race for governor. Along with many leading Black ministers, Al Vann, an African-American power broker based in

Bed-Stuy, was also a key Cuomo ally. Black voters catapulted Mario into the Executive Mansion.

The elder Cuomo served three terms as governor, before losing to an upstate Republican (George Pataki) who made restoring the death penalty his key issue. Andrew then took an executive position with HUD under President Bill Clinton, moving up to become a Cabinet secretary in Arkansas Democrat's second term. Close ties to a president who received large support from Black voters certainly did not hurt the younger Cuomo's reputation. Two days before the June 2025 primary, Clinton endorsed the now-mayoral candidate.

Starting in 2006, in his four consecutive wins for statewide offices, Andrew racked up large numbers of votes in Black communities from Harlem through Central Brooklyn to Southeast Queens. Whether that reflected equal enthusiasm for both Cuomos is an open question, though.

Two weeks before the 2025 mayoral primary, an audience member at a Zohran event in Greenwich Village asked about Cuomo's support from many Black leaders across the city. "I've had many conversations, including with pastors, who've described their endorsement of Andrew Cuomo as an endorsement of Mario's son," Mamdani replied.

According to State Sen. Jabari Brisport, Zohran's DSA comrade, the city's older Black voters generally view "trust" as much more important than "promises" about what a candidate's platform will do for them. Having been "lied to" many times over, Brisport told me, this large swath of the city's electorate views big plans quite skeptically.

Run Zohran Run!

Brisport, whose district spans from Fort Greene and Clinton Hill through Bed-Stuy to Brownsville, observes that many Black voters over fifty supported Cuomo mainly because he was quite familiar to them. Scandals notwithstanding, the former governor's daily televised updates during the pandemic had provided forceful reassurance that Mario's son was looking out for their well-being. As the primary race took shape, Brisport brought Zohran to meet Black clergy and community leaders.

In late April, Zohran spoke to a large number of older Black voters at Medgar Evers College in Crown Heights. Sponsored by the Brooklyn Democratic Party, the event organizers cut a deal with their preferred candidate. Cuomo would indeed make one of his rare public appearances— provided that the format was individual interviews with contenders, not a forum with many figures on stage responding to each other's comments.

Zohran's turn came second, and he began by informing the largely Black audience of a few hundred people that his middle name honors Kwame Nkrumah. The fifteen-minute slot allowed the newcomer to explain his proposals regarding public safety and affordability in response to questions raised by host Ayanna Harry from NY1. Although the crowd gave him a favorable round of applause, it was more like Zohran had hit a solid single than a home run.

The fireworks came at the end of the event, when the former governor took his turn. As he sat down with Harry, a group of youthful, racially diverse protesters charged onto the stage, chanting "Cuomo lies—New Yorkers die," referring to the nursing home scandal during the pandemic. Other than when he got up to shake hands with some supporters, the frontrunner sat passively during the disturbance, which was resolved by the NYPD.

After Cuomo dismissed the dissenters' outburst with a "people in New York City always disagree"-type comment, Harry asked him about his initial campaign theme:

> Harry: *NYPD statistics show that on many serious crimes, the numbers are coming down. The city seems to be getting safer, but a lot of New Yorkers don't feel safer. How do you address that perception issue—and help folks just feel safer?*
>
> Cuomo: *I don't believe it's a perception issue. If I don't feel safe, I don't feel safe. And you saying to me, "You should feel safe because the statistics say I'm safer," that doesn't work for me. Don't tell me that my feeling is wrong, right? My feeling is legitimate because that's what I feel.*

To emphasize the point, the former governor stated that the "random assaults by mentally ill homeless people are one of the prime movers of this feeling of anxiety," which few people would dispute. But his only solution was greater NYPD presence below ground—not the mental health intervention teams Zohran and criminal justice activists advocate.

More problematic was what Cuomo called two "horrendous" incidents that recently happened on the subway— "people getting burned, people dying on subways and then being violated." The high-profile events involving an arson-murder and necrophilia were indeed eye-popping, but they were isolated cases, not indicative of a terrifying pattern.

Like many older voters (of all backgrounds) in the city, Cuomo's view of crime flows directly from the *New York Post*, which sets the table for local TV and radio news. Depending on location, severity, and the backgrounds of the people involved, a single violent incident can create shockwaves across the city.

Prior to joining the race, the suburban candidate clearly ingested plenty of scary headlines. "Dire is the vibe" is how *City & State*'s Holly Pretsky characterized Cuomo's protracted March 1 video statement. "The anxiety rises up in your chest as you're walking down into the subway," claimed the veteran Democrat. "You see it in the empty store fronts, the graffiti, the grime, the migrant influx, the random violence. The city just feels threatening, out of control."

As Ayanna Harry mentioned at the Medgar Evers forum, the city's most important crime number had been trending downwards since Cuomo entered the field, with murders dropping by more than 40 percent from mid-March through mid-April. The frontrunner had banked on the "perception" that the city was besieged by violence. Mario's son wanted voters to fear killers, arsonists, and predators of all kinds so they would view him as their Dark Knight.

Tough luck, Batman.

*

After Cuomo cruised to reelection in 2018, there was chatter among pundits that he might run for president. The governor's closest aide later noted that Mario's pal Joe Biden talked him out of it, with the latter arguing that two moderate candidates would create an opening for a left-winger (either Bernie Sanders or Elizabeth Warren). When the pandemic struck in March 2020, Cuomo seized the national spotlight, scoring an Emmy Award for his daily televised press conferences. Less than eighteen months later, he would resign in disgrace, with the Emmy rescinded.

The downfall started in December 2020, when Lindsey Boylan, a former high-ranking staffer in the Cuomo administration, accused the governor of sexual harassment. According to Boylan, who was in her mid-thirties, Cuomo, then in his early sixties, frequently made comments about her "looks" and unexpectedly kissed her on the lips.

A flurry of accusations from present and past Cuomo staffers ensued. Charlotte Bennett, then in her mid-twenties, accused the governor of asking inappropriate questions about her sex life. Bennett's peer Brittany Commisso said that the state's top executive had fondled her. Karen Hinton, who worked as a HUD press aide for Cuomo, recalled that in 2000, Mario's son made "unethical" physical contact.

In early March 2021, Zohran and his five fellow DSA state legislators were among the early voices calling for Cuomo's resignation. AOC soon followed suit, as did Chuck Schumer, Kirsten Gillibrand and dozens of other mainstream Democrats.

That summer, Attorney General Tish James released a damning report confirming the accusations of eleven women against Cuomo. (A DOJ investigation later brought the number to thirteen.) The governor, the AG's investigators concluded, had engaged in "unwanted touching" that the women viewed as "deeply humiliating and offensive." Rather than face impeachment proceedings, Cuomo opted to resign a few days after James released her report. In a televised address on August 10, the guy who had micro-managed Albany for the past decade stated that "Given the circumstances, the best way I can help now is if I step aside and let government get back to government."

Cuomo apologized to his accusers and to his three daughters, telling the latter that "Your dad made mistakes." The governor's offspring were by no means the only people he cared about. however. "I love New York, and I love you," he assured viewers.

*

The loud calls for Cuomo's resignation did not stem just from the harassment scandal. Early in the pandemic, questions began to swirl about the high rate of deaths in the state's nursing homes. An eleventh-hour provision had been mysteriously inserted into the state budget (due April 1 each year) specifically granting those facilities immunity from pandemic-related lawsuits.

Cuomo, unsurprisingly, had collected significant campaign contributions from the nursing home industry during his time in Albany.[60] The state's large network of elder-care residences already had a checkered reputation—but the pandemic now turned the spotlight on their deadly practices.

In late March 2020, the State Department of Health (which answers to the governor) issued a directive instructing nursing homes to accept and readmit patients diagnosed with Covid-19. This meant that hospitals were sending vulnerable elders back to the shared living facilities, a recipe for disaster. After the lethal impact of the state order became clear in mid-April, Cuomo implausibly claimed that he did not know who issued it. He then declared that nursing homes did not "have the right to object" to the command.

Over 15,000 seniors ultimately died in New York's nursing homes during the pandemic, with over 40% of the fatalities at locations in the city, primarily in Queens, Brooklyn and the Bronx.

Even as Cuomo's daily TV presence elevated his status throughout 2020, critics across the political spectrum blasted his administration's nursing home policies. Janice Dean, a meteorologist on *Fox & Friends* who lost both in her in-laws in elder care facilities during the pandemic, relentlessly denounced Cuomo on social media. Queens assemblyman Ron Kim, a Democrat who lost his uncle, had a high-profile showdown with Cuomo, with the legislator accusing the governor of verbal threats. "No man has ever spoken to me like that in my entire life," Kim told CNN.

---

60   *The Indypendent* (4-23-2020).

Run Zohran Run!

As journalist Ross Barkan explains, the public thus witnessed two competing narratives regarding Cuomo during the pandemic. The governor and his allies (especially his younger brother Chris, then a CNN nightly host) created a "mythos of Cuomo [as] coronavirus conqueror." That competed with the "Cuomo killed grandma" charge amplified by the Murdoch media outlets.[61]

It was up to the millions of New Yorkers trapped at home, with both traditional and social media as their main connections to the world, to decide which story to believe. With boosts from local celebrities including Rosie Perez and Chris Rock (both raised in Brooklyn), Cuomo convinced many people that he would shepherd them out of a very scary crisis.[55]

As Zohran and his team realized, their task was to show that regardless of what happened four years earlier, Cuomo was oblivious to voters' everyday concerns in 2025. Starting with the March presser at Sutton Place, Mamdani demonstrated that he was unafraid to challenge Goliath. In both style and substance, there was also a monumental gap between the two candidates.

Zohran is just under half Cuomo's age but has at least four times more energy. The smiling young guy took the subway, ran the marathon, chatted with voters while walking on city streets, and cheerfully shared playoff fever with excited Knicks fans.

---

61 Ross Barkan, *Cuomo: Return of the Dark Prince* (OR Books, 2025).

Meanwhile, a scowling old dude drove around in his beloved black Dodge Charger, a muscle car favored by suburban teenagers in the 1970s. And the only place Mario's kid seemed comfortable chatting was on the couch in Marcia Kramer's WCBS-TV studio.

*

Zohran joined Brad Lander and seven other candidates at a late March event in Cobble Hill, Brooklyn, near a wall with photos of loved ones who perished in nursing homes. But in general, Cuomo's role in that crisis did not receive much attention during the primary.

That was not the case for the accusations of sexual harassment, however. Lindsey Boylan, the former governor's initial accuser, remained particularly vocal in her condemnation of her former boss. From the day Cuomo entered the race through June 24, Boylan provided constant social media reminders about the misconduct accusations that caused Cuomo to resign.

Cuomo enthusiasts stood by their man, with one ubiquitous agitator slurring Boylan in front of her adolescent daughter on the weekend before the primary. Boylan nonetheless seemed hopeful that her efforts would pay off. On June 23, she advised her daughter that "I and every person I respect is doing all they can to beat this monster and that we are very hopeful today."

Two days earlier, Boylan's fellow Cuomo accuser Charlotte Bennett joined her at a press conference with Lander. As several candidates spotlighted, the former governor's hyper-aggressive legal team, led by powerhouse corporate attorney Rita Glavin, had collected over $60 million in taxpayer-funded legal fees.

Glavin crossed the line for many Cuomo critics by suing to obtain Bennett's gynecological records. That action contributed to Zohran's viral attack on Cuomo at the second televised debate.

Although there were countless mayoral forums held across the city through the winter and spring, Cuomo almost never bothered to attend. While he was required to participate in the two televised debates in June, the veteran pol hardly seemed thrilled to join the discussion.

More surprising is that after four years to workshop his explanations of the nursing home and harassment scandals, Cuomo's answers were meandering and lawyerly.

Goliath may drive a fast car, but he isn't very quick on his feet.

CHAPTER 8
Sticks and Stones

Although Kamala Harris and Chuck Schumer steered the Democratic Party away from Gaza during the 2024 election, Zohran and the DSA continued to pay plenty of attention to the humanitarian nightmare. As Liza Featherstone noted in her *Jacobin* interview with Mamdani at the time of his mayoral launch, Zohran "has been a stalwart supporter for justice in Palestine at a time of immense pressure for elected officials like him to keep their mouths shut on the ongoing genocide there." At the post-October 7 protests, the DSA legislator also had no qualms using the term "genocide" when criticizing Israel and the funding it receives from the U.S.

Prior to his entry into the 2025 race, the candidate told Featherstone, Gaza had already become an issue because of Eric Adams and the NYPD. In early May 2024, following the advice of deep-pocketed Zionists, including hedge-fund billionaire Dan Loeb, the NYPD stormed the Columbia University campus in order to break up a pro-Palestine protest. The police conducted a Fallujah-style door-to-door search in the activist-occupied Hamilton Hall, which the student leaders had renamed Hind's Hall in honor of Hind Rajab, a six-year-old Palestinian girl killed by the Israeli military in Gaza. In the process, a cop fired his weapon into an empty office. The NYPD said it was an accident.

"We could have seen students killed," Mamdani warned Featherstone. Mayor Adams, he continued, "has used his bully pulpit to erase an entire people's humanity, denying calls for a cease-fire. A *cease-fire*," Zohran repeated incredulously.

As journalist Peter Beinart argued the day after Mamdani's primary victory, leading Israel allies such as Loeb and Bill Ackman will lend their considerable financial support to any candidates who pledge "unqualified support" for Israel. Both Cuomo and Adams have no qualms about defending mass slaughter if it helps their political careers. Mamdani and the DSA showed that the next generation of New York City's political leaders would no longer remain silent about Palestine.

Even as Zohran's campaign gained momentum in early 2025, the insurgent's stance on Israel was treated by the media as somehow scandalous. The *New York Post* led the charge, running scores of news stories and opinion pieces that pounced on any past or recent utterance by Zohran that could be construed as antisemitic. The *Post*'s sundry cranky columnists were joined by special guest fellow travelers, including a well-known pro-Israel college basketball coach who visited New York City and took offense at Mamdani's pledge to carry out the International Criminal Court arrest warrant for Bibi Netanyahu.[62]

Cuomo, meanwhile, had joined Netanyahu's legal team defending him before the ICC from arrest. As I detailed in *Drop Site News*, the former New York attorney general announced that he would join the Alan Dershowitz-led retinue in late November 2024, at a Manhattan gathering of Chabad-Lubavitch movement, a powerful ultra-Orthodox Jewish group with close ties to Trump and Israel's current regime. Although the *Post* shared Cuomo's deference to Netanyahu, Rupert Murdoch's house organ did not support Mario's kid, for reasons discussed below.

In sync with the Trump White House, the *Post* cheered on the early March arrest and detention of Columbia University graduate student Mahmoud Khalil, which separated the pro-Palestine leader from his pregnant wife. The Trump administration invoked a McCarthy era-statute that allowed for the revocation of student visas for people deemed to be foreign policy threats.

When border czar Tom Homan, who supported Khalil's arrest, came to Albany a few days afterwards, Zohran angrily confronted him. "Do you believe in the First Amendment?" the assemblyman shouted, garnering

---

62 In criticizing Mamdani "divisiveness," Auburn University's Bruce Pearl offered (on July 3) the highly questionable contention that Alabama "provides an alternative vision: Cherishing faith and country fosters a healthy pluralism that represents America at her best."

national attention. The ACLU, Writers against the War on Gaza, and ousted Columbia Law professor Katherine Franke (an early Zohran for NYC donor) joined Mamdani in denouncing the Trump administration's capricious actions.

The day after his arrest, a *Post* story falsely connected Khalil to Hamas. Two weeks later, the tabloid claimed that the activist had been the "political affairs officer" at UNRWA, the relief agency Israel painted as pro-Hamas. In truth, Khalil had merely done an internship at the large organization, and UNRWA did not have a political affairs officer. The tabloid's approach to Zohran's rise was similarly hostile, with accuracy again viewed as an incidental concern.

*

Zohran's initial appearance on the *Post*'s cover[63] came in early April, by which point the insurgent was polling in second place. "Dangerous Mam," read a large *Post* front-page headline on Wednesday, April 2, which was placed next to an action shot of Zohran running. "They usually have a better pun game," Mamdani told me with a smile when we spoke shortly after his cover debut. "I'm not sure what that one even means." Although the DSA insurgent was still 20-25 points behind Mario's son, he was gaining ground, and the former's support for Palestine was not holding him back.

---

63 Although the *Post*'s website has exponentially more readers than the print edition, the tabloid's front page is still viewed by many within New York City's local political media as an agenda-setter, often influencing local TV news coverage.

Along with the large "Mam" headline and action shot of Zohran, the Murdoch rag included a small pic of Rep. Rashida Tlaib, adding a screenshot of Palestine flag emojis posted in response to the Squad member's recent Zoom call discussing Mamdani's campaign. Veteran columnist Michael Goodwin, a hardcore Trumper, denounced Zohran's support from Brooklyn's prominent Palestinian activist Linda Sarsour and Tlaib. The newspaperman smeared them as "two notorious antisemites," but did not make the same claim regarding Zohran. After the primary, however, Murdoch's hatchet man called the winner "a nepo baby who is a socialist antisemite." Unlike the *Times*, the *Post* minces few words.

In early May, Rupert's crew took aim at Ella Emhoff, another prominent Mamdani backer who is Kamala Harris' stepdaughter and lives in Bushwick. In the *Post*'s view, Emhoff is an "insanely rich nepo-baby" and a hypocrite for supporting a socialist. On Sunday night, May 4, the fashion designer attended a large Mamdani rally at Brooklyn Steel, a music venue in her neighborhood. Ella then shared a clip from the event on Instagram in which she declared her support for Zohran.

In their trash-spewing tirade, Murdoch's deputies declared that Emhoff's support showed that "Zohran 'Man of the People' Mamdani continues to win the hearts of nepo babies and Jew-haters." "To be fair," the editorial claimed, "Emhoff *does* represent a key Mamdani demographic: rich kids from out of town posing as gritty, tough native New Yorkers" (emphasis original). Support from Emhoff—who has advocated for Palestinian causes—illustrated what the *Post* claimed was "central to" Zohran's campaign and to the "coalitional politics of the modern left: rabid antisemit[ism]."

This unhinged attack made me curious about its origins. I asked Michael Benjamin, a member of the *Post* editorial team, whether he wrote the statement. He said no but clarified that "editorials are unsigned but represent the sentiment of the board."

"Why do you ask?" Benjamin queried.

"I'm wondering if my opposition to Israel's war crimes makes me an 'antisemite,'" I replied.

"What war crimes?" Benjamin responded. "War should be brutal and short. Antisemites don't believe in Israel's right to exist."

I was taken aback, but rather than prolong the exchange, I opted to send Benjamin a link to former Human Rights Watch figurehead Kenneth Roth's most insightful June 2024 *New York Review of Books* rundown of Israel's manifold violations of international law. Benjamin acknowledged receipt.[64]

---

64 The day after Zohran's October 23 launch party, Benjamin responded to Asad Dandia's enthusiastic X post about the event by stating "Is it true that no pagers were allowed?", referring to Israel's deadly assaults in Lebanon and Syria in September 2024. As *Semafor*'s Max Tani documented in a post-primary recap, Murdoch's guy later made another pager reference on X regarding Mamdani. According to Andrew Epstein, Zohran frequently brought up Benjamin's "jokes" when speaking to Muslim audiences.

By the end of May, Zohran clearly had the wind in his sails, causing the *Post* board to claim that "antisemitism may be the main reason why Assemblyman Zohran Mamdani is doing so well."

I checked in again with Benjamin, sending him a tweet from *Jewish Daily Forward* reporter Jacob Kornbluh showing Mamdani getting 20% support from the city's Jewish voters in a recent poll (placing Zohran only 11% behind Cuomo, and slightly ahead of Brad Lander). I asked whether such enthusiasm undercut the antisemitism charges against Zohran.

Benjamin responded by calling the 20% of Jews supporting Zohran as the "self-hating ones, who are oversampled" in the poll.

"The 'self-hating ones' who don't like war crimes?" I asked.

"What war crimes?" Benjamin reiterated.

Benjamin (b. 1958, in the Bronx), who is Black and Protestant, thus deployed a twentieth-century slur against liberal Jews. While Mamdani supporters (including yours truly) may find his views appalling, Benjamin, like the rest of his colleagues at the *Post*, at least does not try to hide his opinions.

*

Although the *Post* relentlessly thrashed Mamdani throughout the primary (and well into the summer), Murdoch's team showed no love for Cuomo. Had the powerful outlet backed the former governor, it's conceivable that the race would have been closer.[65]

On Saturday, March 1, the day Cuomo formally launched his mayoral run, the *Post* editorial team deemed him to be "the biggest liar in New York." The board certainly did not like the former governor's handling of the pandemic, particularly the nursing home scandal. Written as a sarcastic piece of advice, the statement further warned young women that Cuomo will "grope you."

What seemed to bother Murdoch's crew most of all was that although he governed as a centrist, Cuomo on occasion tacked left (if he saw the wind blowing that direction). As the editorial mentioned, Cuomo banned fracking and signed progressive criminal justice legislation, including bail reform. Any leftward shifts are anathema to the *Post*, the de facto mission of which is to aid the 1% by keeping the 99% at war with each other. In April, the *New York Times* reported that the former governor was so frustrated with the tabloid's unfavorable coverage that he sought to meet with Rupert Murdoch (b. 1931) to clear the air.

It's not certain whether Cuomo ever got a chance to pull on the Fox patriarch's ear, but he didn't get much favorable treatment from the tabloid down the stretch. As soon as the June 24 primary ended, the *Post* unsuccessfully

---

65 As the eminent U.S. historian Eric Foner has observed, "The great thing about counterfactual (i.e. 'What if...') questions is that there are no wrong answers." Given that the *Post* helped propel Adams in 2021, any show of support from the Murdoch outlet may have helped motivate Cuomo's older voter base.

tried to force the toppled frontrunner into removing his name from the general election ballot. Meanwhile, on Wednesday, June 25, Mayor Eric Adams visited the *Post*'s headquarters in Midtown. The mayor had just denounced Zohran as a "snake-oil salesman for socialism" on *Fox & Friends*, so he was in Murdoch's neighborhood.

*

"Zohran Mamdani is an antisemite!" "His father is antisemitic!" So came the repetitious onslaught of slurs from an extremely aggressive antagonist at a Sunset Park rally on an otherwise beautiful spring afternoon at the beginning of June.

The heckling came from a man who was previously known for waving huge Trump flags at campus protests. RR[66] had recently harassed staffers at an Alexa Avilés campaign event in late May. Zohran, who had been receiving death threats, now had a bodyguard who came with him to Sunset Park.

RR's M.O. is to record video of himself while he gets into people's faces, brushes up against his targets, then tells opponents that they will get arrested for pushing him. It's W.W.E.-type theater, except that RR's venom is not fake.

Zohran had traveled back to scenic Sunset Park, which offers a panoramic sweep of the Statue of Liberty and the downtown Manhattan skyline, in order to give a

---

66 Although RR's name is well-known to the activists he has confronted, it merits no mention here.

pre-canvass pep talk. As scores of volunteers eager to knock on doors for Mamdani and Avilés looked on from the hillside grass, a phalanx of staffers for both campaigns sought to restrain RR while he spewed venom and tried to move toward Zohran.

Clad in combat gear while wearing a black MAGA baseball cap, RR pushed a brave but diminutive young woman out of the way and then mixed it up with a beefier, male Avilés staffer he had previously baited at the May event. After several minutes of skirmishing, the DSA antagonist went to the other side of a fence.

When RR reached into a duffel bag, many of us feared that he was pulling out a gun. Instead, it was a megaphone, enabling the loudmouth to amplify his vitriol. "You're all a bunch of socialists!" was one of the few accurate things RR shouted, provoking a few chuckles. "God bless Trump!" he screamed.

It was clear to everyone on-hand that RR was almost certainly a habitual consumer of Murdoch bile. At the event I asked the candidate about an article that had been on the *Post* site since the previous afternoon. Zohran's answer surprised me.

"Did you see the story about Stringer's call for the NYPD to partner with the ADL?" I inquired, referring to one of his competitor's flailing attempts to score points with conservative Jewish Democrats by letting the far-right ADL decide which social media posts are antisemitic and may pose imminent danger.

"Really? I haven't seen it," Zohran replied, leading me to surmise that, unlike most candidates, Mamdani's morning routine did not include checking out who Murdoch's minions were bashing or hyping that day.

According to Andrew Epstein, Zohran's news consumption during the primary followed no clear pattern. Sometimes he knew very specific details buried deep in stories from an assortment of outlets. Other times he was unaware of coverage that many in his inner circle followed closely. Because "the volume of *Post* stuff about Zohran was so intense," Andrew explains, "we often opted not to call his attention to the latest attack." Although Mamdani sometimes looked at the *Post,* Epstein says the candidate did not do so "obsessively."

Other than denounce Zohran, it's not clear what the DSA hater had hoped to accomplish that Sunday afternoon in Sunset Park. Although his attacks surely could be heard in areas surrounding the park, RR directed them towards Mamdani and Avilés volunteers who had decided to spend their weekend leisure time knocking on voters' doors.

As RR continued to harangue, I asked a thirty-something male canvasser wearing a patterned short-sleeve button-down shirt the following question: "Do you think this dude reads the *New York Post*?"

"I think he writes it," the millennial quipped, without missing a beat.

CHAPTER 9
A Creative Class

A successful long-shot election campaign in a sizable race requires six major ingredients: a compelling candidate, a timely message, the necessary funding, a strong field operation, media savvy, and an innovative creative design team.

Zohran clearly had chops, and his agenda met the moment. Although he was not the only candidate with substantial funds, Mamdani's volunteer army was unmatched. From day one, no rival contender came even remotely close to matching Zohran for NYC's overall media game. Zohran's marketing crew was also nothing if not state of the art (or craft). Meanwhile, in sync with its candidate, Team Cuomo's campaign materials were extremely yesterday.

One day after Mamdani's primary triumph, *New York* magazine's city editor Christopher Bonanos assessed the winning campaign's graphic design output. The veteran journalist heaped praise on Mamdani's team. By contrast,

Run Zohran Run!

Bonanos observed, "I cannot for the life of me tell you what Andrew Cuomo's logotype looks like."

Whereas Cuomo's logo stuck with the familiar red, white and blue scheme, Zohran's palate was far from "conventional," explained Bonanos. Mamdani's main signage discarded the first two parts of the trinity altogether, and—according to designer Aneesh Bhoopathy—the campaign's most-used blue backdrop verged slightly toward violet.

A former Queens resident (now living in Philly), Bhoopathy told Bonanos that his firm's "mood board was definitely New York iconography: taxicab yellow, MetroCard primary colors, bodega awnings, stuff people are familiar with in the New York street." The "ZOHRAN" lettering in the logo found on the campaign's posters, buttons, and bandannas was hand-drawn, paying homage to a typeface named Boheld. Set against the blue backdrop, the orange-lined yellow lettering was eye-catching, the mustard tinge within the body of each letter enhancing the appeal.

Zohran was an early teen when social media first debuted. Many of his younger followers have grown up in a world in which images vastly outweigh the power of the written word. While it would be shocking if a millennial mayoral candidate did not have compelling graphics, it's not at all surprising that Cuomo ignored the importance of his campaign's visual appeal, or lack thereof.

Bhoopathy, meanwhile, hit what many in the U.S. would call a home run, although cricket devotees might refer to it as a "sixer."

*

Rather than send out several rounds of glossy mailers to likely primary voters, Mamdani's legions of volunteers aimed to make direct contact with them. And if no one answered, the door-knocker would leave campaign lit. At my co-op apartment building in Sunset Park, I returned home at least four times and found materials for Mamdani and/or DSA Councilwoman Alexa Avilés either on my doorknob or under my front door. Such direct outreach creates a far greater chance that the prospective voter will actually look at the material. When oversized materials get stuffed into small mailboxes, they simply create clutter. Only politics geeks like me are likely to pay attention to the declarations for or against countless candidates.

Zohran's lit left by canvassers also stood out for its stellar design. One door-handle piece featured an action pic of the candidate holding a microphone, placed above the campaign's stylish logo in orange against a solid blue background (the color scheme of the New York Mets). In yellow, the statement encouraged voters to "Rank Zohran #1 for a city you can <u>afford</u>," with the final word in red.

The handbill further listed Zohran's key platform planks, then showed pics of endorsers AOC and Rep. Nydia Velázquez, along with the logos of the DSA, the Working Families Party, and DC 37, the large union of city government clerical workers. It concluded with poll site info and a photo of a smiling Zohran. That is a lot of campaign info to pack into a single piece of campaign lit, but the presentation made it quite visually appealing.

The reverse side of the same piece was in Spanish, with a new top photo showing Zohran with Avilés and fellow DSA

Run Zohran Run!

lawmaker Marcela Mitaynes as well as Brooklyn Borough President Antonio Reynoso. Sunset Park's diverse Spanish-speaking population includes many Puerto Ricans (e.g. Avilés) and Dominicans (who may identify with Reynoso). Until 2022, Velázquez represented the area in Congress.

Stylish and fluent, Zohran's campaign lit reinforced the candidate's upbeat message. It was also produced and paid for by the insurgent's own team, via public funding amassed overwhelmingly with small donations from teachers, health care workers, and sundry creative professionals. Cuomo's big-money backers got much less bang for their bucks.

*

After he entered the race in March, Cuomo quickly amassed $4 million, spurred by hundreds of maximum donations ($2,100) from people who clearly are not educators or health care staffers. By the end of the primary, the frontrunner received over $4 million in matching funds. About half of the $5.5 million Cuomo's campaign doled out was for TV ads.

Dark money did most of the talking on Cuomo's behalf. Although New York City has a quite progressive matching funds program, outside spending for candidates cannot be restricted (because of *Citizens United*). The city's Campaign Finance Board tracks the money flow from PACs.

Fix the City, the lead PAC supporting Cuomo, hauled in just over $25 million by June 30, almost entirely from

1% donors or major corporations. Michael Bloomberg blazed the money trail, dumping $8.3 million into the PAC's coffers. DoorDash, angry about pro-delivery worker measures recently passed by the City Council, made a down payment of a million bucks on Cuomo. Three people connected to the Estée Lauder cosmetics empire also delivered a combined $1 million.

Billionaire financiers Bill Ackman and Daniel Loeb, both leading Israel hawks, kicked in $500,000 and $350,000, respectively, with Loeb also spearheading Cuomo's campaign fundraising. Oil baron John B. Hess ponied up $500,000 to Fix the City and entertainment mogul Barry Diller dropped $250,000.

Over fifteen high-rollers matched Diller's ante. Several leading real estate developers joined that list, including those responsible for Manhattan "supertall" skyscrapers and large luxury condo projects on the Brooklyn waterfront.[67] By the time polls opened on June 24, Fix the City had spent over $20.5 million[68] on everything from taxi-cab billboards to text messages. Mailboxes across the five boroughs overflowed with pro-Cuomo campaign literature. So many different candidates distribute mailers during election season that the impact of any single glossy piece seems minimal, especially the generic material produced on Cuomo's behalf.

---

67 Alice Walton, the Walmart heiress, was the most recognizable name among the 35 or so donors giving between $100-$250,000.
68 By the end of the primary, the PAC spent roughly $22.4 million, presumably keeping $2.7 million to spend on the general election. A handful of other groups spent over a combined $4 million more.

Despite its deep reservoir of funds, Fix the City did not invest in an even minimally creative ad creation team. Team Cuomo's marketing output was cartoonishly retrograde, which was especially surprising given that Bloomberg, the Lauders, and Barry Diller surely know a few inventive folks on Madison Avenue.

The gist of Fix the City's output was stridently anti-Mamdani. Because of his criticisms of Israel, his past support for defunding the NYPD, and his socialist worldview, Zohran needed to be stopped. The PAC's arguments regarding why voters should support their candidate were far less affirmative. "For a safe and more affordable NYC, vote Cuomo," urged Fix the City in one of its countless mailers. The handbill's front side further included the PAC's preferred photo of the veteran Democrat, in which the wincing former governor sports a furrowed brow and stern expression. The flip-side of the same glossy mailer warns "YOU MUST VOTE TO STOP ZOHRAN MAMDANI'S RADICAL PLANS." No policy details accompanied the generic rally cries.

In smaller font, "We Demand Defund the NYPD" is superimposed over a photo of a young Zohran wearing a non-Western shirt. In a second, more recent picture, the less-exoticized insurgent candidate holds a microphone. A deceptive *New York Post* quote placed between the two shots of the candidate declares that "Mamdani wants to take 'police out of high-crime areas.'"[69]

---

69 The quote is taken from an interview in which a Muslim female host asks a younger Zohran about the aggressive actions of police in "high-crime areas." Mamdani responds by discussing the need

The PAC's attacks never invoked *All in the Family*'s Archie Bunker, but the specter of the archetypal Queens working-class bigot of the 1970s hovered. Legally, the Cuomo campaign could not coordinate with Fix the City, although candidates can denounce slurs made on their behalf, which Mario's son never did.

Yet in presenting their guy from Queens a sneering modern-day Archie, Fix the City may have unwittingly built support for a halal version of "Meathead," Bunker's lefty son-in-law.

*

Fix the City spent roughly $6.5 million running TV and internet ads from early March through mid-May. They were more polished and contemporary than the PAC's other productions. Two initial 30-second TV spots featured Cuomo interacting with older, mainly Black folks and touted his record.

Starting in early June, the Fix team started to focus almost entirely on attacking Cuomo's fast-ascending rival, spending over $7 million on a new round of TV and internet placements (and another $7 million or so on mailers, etc.). Mamdani, the ads reiterated, was a "radical" and "a risk we can't afford" who continued to support defunding the police.

As primary day neared, Team Cuomo's TV spots also played up the *New York Times* editorial board's denunciations of

---

for more community intervention teams but does not actually say that cops should play no role.

the newcomer. The same crew of mixed-race purported Cuomo fans who appeared in the initial ads cropped up again in the later round. The former governor spent such a minimal amount of time interacting with voters that there was little other footage to use.

It's hard to grab someone's attention with a mass text message, no matter how exciting the candidate might be. Zohran for NYC's blasts also lacked punch, primarily because an automated statement is an impersonal form of contact. Fix the City's spam was nonetheless revealing.

After a lengthy paragraph touting the former governor's "experience," one of the PAC's text missives read, "In these uncertain times, we must STOP Zohran Mamdani." The alert offered no explanation as to why Zohran posed such a dire threat. One potential, unintended effect of such a statement might have been to spur an unfamiliar voter to seek out more details about the charismatic new contender.

Although "robo-texts" may be ignored or viewed simply as a nuisance by recipients, they're very cheap, enabling campaigns or outside spenders to send two million messages for well under $100,000. They also can target specific subsets of voters. Like their preferred candidate, Fix the City's communiques on election day were a throwback to New York City's tribal politics of yesteryear.

In a message aimed at the "NYT audience,"[70] a robot identifying as "Beth" started by declaring that the "*New*

---

70 The city's Campaign Finance Board website includes copies of the materials distributed by outside spending groups.

Theodore Hamm

York Times, *Daily News* and *New York Post* all agree: DO NOT RANK MAMDANI." In the late twentieth century, such unanimity likely would have knocked out an upstart candidate. But unlike the primary just four years before, pronouncements by the *Times* and *Post* carried no weight in June 2025.

Fix the City's election-day missives provided a theater of the absurd. In reaching out to "working-class voters" (presumably white ethnics), "Harry" claimed that his wife is terribly afraid of Mamdani. Jewish voters, meanwhile, heard from "Rachel, for one last time, I promise!" A purportedly Black texter named "Dave" began his message by telling recipients that "I couldn't stay away!"

The various PAC attacks sought to deflate Zohran's momentum, but it is tricky to gauge the impact of the multi-pronged effort. Amid the deluge of smears, polls showed steadily increasing support for Mamdani. Cuomo gained no ground from the many millions of dollars spent on his behalf.

*

Fix the City's egregious sleaze spawned a viral backlash against the mix of anti-Muslim bigotry and bullying funded by the city elite. On June 11, the day before the second televised debate, Jacob Kornbluh, senior political reporter for the *Forward*, posted what appeared to be a new Fix the City mailer. The content—which asserted that Mamdani "rejects" Israel and "Jewish rights" (as well the NYPD and capitalism)—was incendiary, but a clumsily photoshopped thickening and darkening of Mamdani's beard caused the story to blow up.

Mamdani seized the opportunity to connect Cuomo's elite donors to an obvious Islamophobic hit job. Just before noon on June 12, the insurgent's team released a statement in which Zohran declared that "Andrew Cuomo's SuperPAC—funded by the same billionaires that elected Donald Trump—is trying to buy this election through fear-mongering and ignorance."

A Fix the City spokeswoman insisted that the mailer with the distorted beard was a rejected mock-up that never circulated. Regardless, Team Cuomo's slimy tactics ended up benefiting Mamdani, who pointedly invoked the distorted mailer in that night's debate.

On the weekend before the primary, with the trendlines during early voting clearly favoring Zohran, the flailing Cuomo crew solicited headline-making endorsements from two members of the Democratic Party's old guard. First up was Jim Clyburn, the seventeen-term House member from South Carolina who helped snuff out Bernie Sanders' 2020 presidential bid. Next was Mario Cuomo's pal Bill Clinton, who had made Andrew a member of his Cabinet.

Favorable legacy media coverage notwithstanding, neither Democratic pillar's backing suggested that Cuomo might be the candidate of the future. But what is most notable is how the high-profile plugs reached voters. Team Cuomo touted the fact that Clyburn and Clinton had recorded robocalls, which harkened back to the pre-cellphone era.

Clyburn's Southern drawl may have appealed to some older Black voters; and although his voice sounds a bit shaky these days, there is no mistaking Bill Clinton's familiar inflections. But how many voters picked up the phone, listened to the entire call—and felt inspired to vote for Cuomo—is an open question.

When Cuomo visited Brooklyn's large Christian Cultural Center on the Sunday before the primary, the congregation responded enthusiastically to mention of Clinton's support. Reverend A.R. Bernard, a powerful off-stage player in city politics, told a *New York Times* reporter that Cuomo spoke "brilliantly" for five minutes, during which he slammed the DSA. But instead of interacting with the congregation after his remarks, the former governor exited. In general, Cuomo "was not on the streets, where the people are," observed Rev. Bernard. "Maybe we have to be careful when we assume that we've got enough reputation, history, and gravitas to float."[71]

As Bernard acidly noted, even when he showed up to a friendly room, Mario's son seemed temperamentally unwilling to engage with voters. After his humiliating primary defeat, Cuomo appeared to realize that he needed to interact with people more. He hit the streets in casual clothes and shook a lot of hands. Cuomo's new approach to the general election initially yielded mixed results. As CNN's Gloria Pazmino reported in late July, when the candidate visited a public housing site in East Harlem, a man "pulled Cuomo in for a handshake, took

---

71 As quoted by Nicholas Fandos on X (6-27-2025).

out his phone for a selfie, and as the former three-term governor of New York smiled for the camera, told him, 'I can't wait to watch you lose again.'"

*

Like the veteran Democrat himself, Cuomo's campaign team and Fix the City projected a downbeat, dreary vision of the future. Mamdani and his millennial crew were the polar opposite. Team Zohran projected future vs. past, optimism vs. cynicism, vitality vs. fatigue.

On the weekend before the primary, Cuomo talked up his handling of Superstorm Sandy, which happened thirteen years earlier. "This is not the time for on-the-job training," he insisted. It was his umpteenth attempt to call attention to Mamdani's lack of executive experience. In truth, Cuomo's handling of Sandy had sparked much criticism.[72] As his campaign showed, disaster management is not Cuomo's strong suit.

---

72 As Zephyr Teachout reminded her X followers (6-24-2025), during Sandy residents of Long Island experienced extended power outages, sparking criticism of Cuomo and other state officials for their poor communication regarding when area electricity would be restored.

CHAPTER 10
Buckle Up

"Mamdani passes on condemning the Holocaust," read the alarming subject line of an influential morning newsletter from *Politico*'s New York Playbook on Friday, May 16. Thus began a whirlwind ride for Zohran, which did not stop until his victory party forty nights later. The journey saw Mamdani's stance on Israel move to the center of the race for mayor of New York City.

One night earlier, the insurgent candidate had appeared at a mayoral forum at the Public Theater near Astor Place hosted by the left-leaning publications *Hell Gate* and *New York Focus*. When Mamdani exited the stage prior to the other two candidates (chipper Brad Lander and very droll Scott Stringer),[73] those of us in attendance wondered where the DSA's man headed off to.

---

73 Asked to name their favorite New York City films, Mamdani answered *Do the Right Thing*, Lander said *Anora*, and Stringer

Run Zohran Run!

The next morning, as seen on his campaign socials, Zohran had zipped from the East Village to Xanadu, a roller rink in Bushwick. There, he took a panoramic selfie video that showed hundreds of wildly enthusiastic supporters in the house. It must have been dizzying for Mamdani to wake up to *Politico*'s Holocaust sucker punch. Yet while Zohran's Zionist critics turned up the heat, some of the insurgent candidate's pro-Palestine allies accused him of watering down his stance towards Israel.

Politico's buzzy Holocaust headline was not paired with a coherent story, but the *New York Post* and its social media devotees eagerly helped amplify it. Each year, the New York legislature approves scores of resolutions on subjects ranging from important historical events to current controversies including the use of A.I. The statements are passed via voice vote. Zohran, in fact, affirmed his support for this year's Holocaust resolution, as he had done previously. But unlike in past years, Mamdani was not a co-sponsor of the 2025 resolution.

As Zohran explained in a video statement recorded later on May 16, he decided at the outset of this year not to co--sponsor any resolutions because he and his fellow legislators are inundated with them. Although *Politico*'s coverage of Mamdani had not been favorable up to this point, it was now adopting the Murdoch organ's smear tactics.

"I am not a supporter of Zohran Mamdani but the notion that his non-sponsorship of the Holocaust resolution means

---

(b. 1960) said *Taxi Driver*, apparently forgetting that Travis Bickle (Robert DeNiro) tries to assassinate a political candidate.

anything is disconnected from what goes on in Albany," Assemblyman Micah Lasher posted on X two days after the story went viral. A Jewish Democrat representing the Upper West Side, Lasher noted that he and his colleagues get "dozens of emails every day" about proclamations of all kinds, and that he finds the "resolution business to be rather silly."

The mundane facts mattered little to *Politico*, the *Post*, or kindred forces. Since 2021, *Politico* has been owned by German publisher Axel Springer, a stridently pro-Israel media powerhouse.[74] In a May 19 editorial, *AM NY*, a free morning paper owned by a longtime Cuomo ally, inanely (and inaccurately) declared that Zohran's unwillingness to condemn "the horrors of the Holocaust in writing and with a vote on the floor" disqualified him.

New York City was experiencing a twenty-first-century outbreak of what Dickens famously called "an age of foolishness."

*

Andrew Epstein, Zohran's communications director during the primary, vividly recalls his own reaction to *Politico*'s Holocaust smear. "I said, 'Wtf?' and started firing off texts and emails," explained Andrew, who is in his late thirties and lives near Zohran in Astoria. Along with Mamdani's then-political director Julian Gerson and the campaign's media strategist Morris Katz, Andrew is Jewish.

---

74 See Ari Paul, "Politico Staff Must Toe New Owner's Line—Including Endorsing Israel," *FAIR* (11-25-2021).

Run Zohran Run!

The same *Politico* hit job called attention to a second pro-Israel resolution in the assembly that Zohran did not support. Later that Friday morning, Zohran held a presser aimed at spotlighting his less-sensational plans to help small businesses in the city. After Mamdani opened the floor (actually, the sidewalk) to questions, reporters asked, "Do you support Israel's right to exist?"

"Yes, I do support Israel's right to exist as a state," Zohran replied. On social media, numerous millennial Mamdani backers began to ridicule the media's relentless focus on Israel. Even when he stated his positions clearly, Zohran was portrayed as somehow evasive.

Along with Epstein and campaign videographer Donald Borenstein, Zohran spent that Friday afternoon filming the insurgent's response video. That night, Andrew and Donald went out to dinner.

When Andrew returned home to Astoria around 10:30 p.m., he got a call from Zohran. The tireless contender wanted his comms guy to join him outside Madison Square Garden, where the Knicks had just finished off their arch-rival Celtics and fans were celebrating like they'd won the NBA title.

Earlier that week, Zohran posted a clip of himself wearing a Knicks cap backwards at a watch party outside of the Garden. A middle-aged white guy in a sleeveless shirt had his right arm around the candidate, while his left index finger pointed to the multi-colored Knicks basketball spinning rapidly on the candidate's head. "Here we are," Zohran said playfully. "We're spinning a ball." It was a memorable moment that did well across platforms. Spontaneity yields results.

Andrew journeyed back from Astoria and met up with campaign aid Spencer Goldberg and Zohran, the only person outside the Garden sporting a suit and tie. The upbeat mayoral hopeful used his lapel mic to interview an assortment of young male fans. Nearly everyone at such gatherings is a social media maven, and many are aspiring performers. "I'm feeling impeccable," said a large, likely Eastern European guy in his twenties. A 21-year-old Latino jumped in to say he would be voting for Zohran. A rotund Black guy, clad in a matching Knicks jersey and beanie, launched into a comedy routine. To the Pacers (the Knicks' next-round opponent), the twenty-something offered fake advance condolences: "I'm so sorry. I'm so sorry…for absolutely nothing!" he yelled at the camera, with his pals roaring behind him and Zohran laughing along.

Andrew returned home, edited the footage and posted clips on the campaign's platforms at 3:15 a.m. A day that began with the Holocaust attack ended on a boisterous note. Amid the madness, Zohran did not stop having fun, suggesting that hate sometimes can be counteracted by ignoring it.

While the insurgent candidate was out on the streets with Knicks fans, his name, face, and message reached people watching at home or in bars. According to Elle Bisgaard-Church, Zohran for NYC's campaign manager during the primary, "We made a massive investment in visibility

Run Zohran Run!

during the Knicks playoff run, understanding that a victory would be dependent on a feeling of joy and possibility."[75]

Starting in late April, Zohran's campaign was the first to hit the airwaves, with its initial ad debuting during a Knicks early playoff game. Produced by Fight Agency, run by Democratic consultant Rebecca Katz,[76] the initial 30-second spot was a state-of-the-craft mix of campaign messaging and criticism of Cuomo, Adams, and their billionaire funders. Another ad that aired later in the Knicks run showed Zohran walking up to tenants and informing them about his rent freeze plan. With New York City apartment buildings providing the stage, the spot evoked *West Side Story*. Here, Zohran was straightforward, not playful. Rather than sing and dance, Mr. Cardamom played it straight.

The Knicks' playoff run eventually flamed out, but Zohran's quest for the title continued. With polls showing the insurgent gaining increasing strength, Mamdani soon faced new foes.

*

At the same time as the Israel controversies blew up, Zohran gained increasing support from city residents. Taken in the first week of May, a Marist College survey of nearly 3,400 likely Democratic voters showed Cuomo leading the second-place Mamdani by 37-18%, with the

---

75 After the primary, Bisgaard-Church became Mamdani's senior advisor.
76 Katz is no relation to Mamdani's media strategist Morris Katz, although the latter also works for Fight Agency.

frontrunner not reaching the necessary 50% until the fifth round of ranked-choice tabulations.

Between May 14 and 18, Workbench Strategy, a progressive research firm retained by the Mamdani campaign, conducted an internal poll that showed Cuomo up 41-28% in round one and not prevailing until round seven. Because they are commissioned by specific candidates, internal polls should be taken with a grain of salt. The Workbench sample size was also only 500 likely voters. The mid-May findings nonetheless started to make an upset win for Zohran seem realistic. His momentum was growing fast.

A few nights after *Politico*'s hit piece, Zohran spoke in Brooklyn's Gowanus at an issue launch party for *Acacia*, a progressive Muslim magazine that debuted in 2024. After the candidate's remarks received a friendly reception, a Palestinian American activist named Anas Saleh angrily confronted Mamdani.

Saleh pointedly accused the candidate of "being hypocritical" when calling for "Free Palestine while saying Israel has a right to exist." The activist said that he had family in Palestine who were under attack, insisting that "Israel does not have the right to exist." The candidate heard him out, but Saleh exited before Mamdani could reply.

Palestinian American Muslim leader Nerdeen Kiswani, the Bay Ridge-based founder of Within Our Lifetime, promoted Saleh's statements on social media. In Kiswani's view, Zohran "never should have" affirmed support for the colonizer's statehood. Mamdani, Kiswani argued, was "trying to appease genocidal maniacs."

As I explained in *Drop Site News*, Zohran responded by addressing concerns about his position directly. The night after the Saleh confrontation, Zohran attended a trans community town hall hosted by Park Slope-based Ceyenne Doroshow, a leading Black activist. Many attendees had participated in Palestine solidarity protests.

Prior to detailing his plans to defend trans rights as mayor, Zohran told the gathering that he wanted "to address something I know is on many of your minds." The candidate assured the group that his position on "Palestinian human rights, liberation, and Gaza" had not changed.

"I will not walk away from my principles or my track record," Zohran continued. "And I don't believe any of us can look away while Israeli war crimes continue to escalate, and thousands of children are being slaughtered." He then reaffirmed his support for BDS and spoke about his "Not on Our Dime" legislation that strips tax-exempt status from New York nonprofits that aid Israel's war crimes.

Andrew Epstein, meanwhile, issued a statement stressing that "Zohran has been consistent in his belief that Israel has the right to exist [with] a responsibility to adhere to international law, and that he supports non-violent movements to ensure compliance with that law."

Rather than modify his support for Palestinian rights, or try to mollify his anti-Israel critics, the DSA candidate remained steadfast. This meant that he was now incurring fire from two different directions, although one side's arsenal contained far heavier artillery.

*

As June opened, Zohran was clearly ascending. But it still remained hard to project victory. I checked in with New York City's next-gen vote wiz Michael Lange, who served as an adviser to Mamdani's campaign.

Eric Adams received 290,000 first-place votes in the 2021 primary, so I asked Lange whether he thought 250,000 was attainable for Zohran. "Yes, I think he can," Michael said, "but turnout would need to exceed one million." The insurgent had been polling well in Brooklyn and stood to collect plenty of votes in Northwest Queens. But as Lange noted, Mamdani couldn't win without racking up large totals in Manhattan.

Late on Monday night, June 2, a far-right city councilwoman from Queens took aim at Zohran. Vickie Paladino (b. 1954), one of six Republican members on the 51-seat body, is a hard-core Trumper who represents a northern Queens neighborhood called Whitestone, the population of which happens to be quite white.

That evening, Paladino's team[77] appeared to have conducted a very deep dive into Mamdani's tweets from 2019. Lo and behold, they found something "damning." The councilwoman shared it with her 33,000 followers on X.

As the 2020 presidential race took shape, Zohran had tweeted three photos of himself from Bernie Sanders' 2016 campaign, including one in which he and Nina Turner

---

77 When the Proud Boys-aligned Paladino first ran for state senate in 2018, her son Thomas Paladino, Jr., then 41, told *Gothamist* (10-17-2018) that he handled his mom's social media accounts.

jointly held a small Bernie sign. Above the pics, the tweet from the aspiring assemblymember read:

> *I couldn't vote for @BernieSanders in 2016 because I wasn't a citizen yet, but I can't wait for my first presidential vote to be for him in 2020.*
>
> *And I'm even more excited to share a ballot with him and help build the political revolution from Albany to Washington.*

Although Mamdani, who became a dual U.S.-Ugandan citizen in 2018, expressed pride in exercising his right to vote, Paladino seized the opportunity to stoke Birtherist hate. At least one guy from Queens surely approved when Paladino declared:

> *Let's just talk about how insane it is to elect someone to any major office who hasn't even been a US citizen for ten years—much less a radical leftist who actually hates everything about the country and is here specifically to undermine everything we've ever been about.*
> *Deport.*

The one-word second paragraph furnished Paladino's crystal-clear message.

In New York City's not-distant past, any comparable display of nativist bigotry toward immigrants by a prominent figure would have been roundly condemned. Editorial boards would call foul, religious and civic leaders would demand an apology, and there would be a loud chorus of calls for the hatemonger to resign.

"Everyone should denounce this," veteran civil rights attorney Norman Siegel (b. 1943) told me at the time. Although Mamdani and his fellow Democratic candidates blasted Paladino, good government groups, faith leaders, and editorial boards mostly remained silent.

The *New York Times* ran a story that foregrounded Zohran's steadfast response: "Death threats. Islamophobic bigotry. Now a sitting councilmember calling for my deportation. Enough. This is what Trump and his sycophants have wrought." Brad Lander offered similar criticism, as did Adrienne Adams, Andrew Cuomo and a few other contenders. But that was about it.

At its midway point, the *Times* report took a curious detour: "Mr. Cuomo is a staunch supporter of Israel; Mr. Mamdani uses the term 'genocide' to describe Israel's actions against Gaza." For good measure, the "paper of record" then tossed Zohran's support for BDS into the mix.

Although Paladino did not mention the Middle East conflict when slamming Zohran, the *Times* made sure to inform readers that the councilwoman is a "strong supporter of Israel." Moreover, the story matter-of-factly noted that, in May 2024, the Whitestone warrior had called pro-Palestine campus protesters "monsters" who need to be "slayed."

"This incident illustrates perfectly the need for President Trump's mass deportation policy," Paladino said in defense of her Mamdani attack. The salty demagogue sought to remove "future Zohrans" from the U.S. "before they have a chance to take root in America."

Run Zohran Run!

With all due respect, ma'am, that ship has sailed. Zohran scored massive support from young voters, who are not full of yesterday's bigotry.

Not long ago, the *Times* editorial board paid close attention to goings-on in New York City. But these days it doesn't even matter to this esteemed body if the NYPD fires a weapon into a college campus office. More surprising than the *Times* board's silence regarding Paladino's incendiary statements is that the *Post* ignored them.

Paladino typically does not need to do much to get coverage in the Murdoch rag. In mid-May, her social media diatribe about the city's composting plan—in which she argued that the small kitchen buckets used in the program worked better as "beer coolers"—earned her a *Post* puff piece. It's not clear why the tabloid ignored her crusade against Zohran, but it's hard to believe that Murdoch's crew disagreed with it.

At City Hall, Mayor Adams appeared to be troubled by the denounce Paladino/support Mamdani binary, so he sought a third option. The mayor, who famously declared that the migrant crisis will "destroy New York City," and claimed that he faced federal corruption charges because he criticized the Biden White House on the issue, did not want to sound too pro-immigration or in any way anti-Trump.

"We should all tone down our rhetoric," Adams said, limply advising New Yorkers to avoid "meanspirited, hateful language." News flash: Nobody listened.

CHAPTER 11
It's Getting Hot

In late May, it was easy to see why Zohran's foes were getting nervous.

An Emerson College Poll, co-sponsored by New York City local news station PIX11 and the Beltway publication *The Hill*, now showed Cuomo not winning until the tenth ranked-choice round. "Could Andrew Cuomo Lose NYC Mayoral Primary to Democratic Socialist Zohran Mamdani?" asked the *Forbes* Breaking News Channel on YouTube.

On Monday morning, June 2, Zohran's campaign rolled out a big endorsement. State Senator John Liu, New York's first Asian American citywide elected official (as comptroller, in office from 2010-2013). Born in Taiwan (in 1967), Liu and his family came to the U.S. when he was a young child. Liu represents the heavily Asian Queens neighborhoods of Flushing and Bayside, just south of

Run Zohran Run!

Paladino's council district.[78] The former comptroller—who clashed with Mayor Bloomberg and ran for mayor as a left populist in 2013—is also a widely respected figure in various ethnic enclaves across the city.

"As a fellow immigrant to this city at a young age, [and] an Asian American," Liu said at the endorsement presser outside City Hall, he and Zohran could identify with "the struggles that our communities go through and the need for a focus on education and economic empowerment." Liu further noted that the insurgent's small-donation fundraising showed that Mamdani was not "beholden to monied interests" and "doesn't owe anybody anything."

Liu nonetheless stressed that while he fully backed his fellow Queens lawmaker's bid for mayor, the two have a "big disagreement" about Israel-Palestine. Somewhat paradoxically, Liu's not-exactly progressive pro-Israel position opened up new terrain of support for Zohran, informing older voters with concerns about Mamdani's pro-Palestine stance that they could still support the newcomer.

Outlets seeking to keep Israel at the center of the mayoral campaign treated Liu's endorsement in a different light, however. "Pro-Israel pol backs Zohran, with reservations," read the headline on *Politico*'s New York Playbook.

Mamdani's campaign, meanwhile, created its own stylish coverage of Liu's announcement, starting with the two

---

78 In the aforementioned 2018 race for state senate, Liu trounced Paladino.

figures walking up the subway steps at City Hall. The video gained strong traction on TikTok and Instagram.

Two weeks later, Zohran posted a dazzling clip of city councilman Chi Ossé (who was born in 1998 and raised in a Haitian-American household in Brooklyn) and Liu explaining their support for Mamdani in Mandarin. Social media is made to be shared, and it can span generations. "My 89-year-old mother loved it!" activist and book editor Andy Hsiao told me regarding the Ossé-Liu exchange.

Zohran's manifest ability to control his own narrative maximized his gain from Liu's endorsement. The same event was thus viewed quite differently by mainstream media audiences versus those seeing it through the candidate's own channels.

From a campaign's perspective, such command is a quite potent weapon. In Journalism 101, we instruct students that, in theory, political media should inform readers, not serve powerful interests. Amid Mamdani's rise, several outlets appeared to be aiding Israel's attempt to muzzle all of its critics. But the effort seems to have backfired. A very large number of Democratic voters shared the DSA candidate's pro-Palestine views—and countless others did not view support for Israel as a major concern.

Given the endless barrage of smear pieces against Zohran, who can fault him for telling his own story?

*

On the same Monday in which Liu endorsed Zohran and Paladino called for the insurgent's deportation, a third, less-noticed event illustrated the new terrain of New York City politics. That evening, two of the city's most venerable civil rights organizations, the NYCLU and the NAACP (New York chapter), sponsored a well-attended forum for mayoral candidates.

Presidential candidate Abraham Lincoln, abolitionist figurehead Frederick Douglass, and President Barack Obama have all taken the stage at the Great Hall at Cooper Union. In 1993, Governor Mario Cuomo introduced President Bill Clinton at an event there. On June 2, 2025, Mario's son evidently needed to be somewhere else.

Zohran and seven fellow candidates opted to join the conversation. No-show Cuomo may not have many enthusiasts among the NYCLU crowd, but he was counting on the NAACP's older Black members to help put him in City Hall. Only the longstanding Harlem-based *Amsterdam News* covered the event. The article's mention of Cuomo's unexplained absence likely raised at least a few eyebrows.

The lack of widespread media coverage—or criticism—of the frontrunner's slight again showed that the old rules of city politics no longer applied. Cuomo cynically but correctly calculated that since he had already blown off most candidate forums, the media would not pay attention to yet another non-appearance. And civic organizations meant very little to him.

Because of his participation in the city's campaign finance program, Cuomo was required to attend the two televised debates, the first of which was slated for Wednesday,

June 4. Whether in first or second place, or very far behind, in the polls, candidates started laying the groundwork for the first showdown.

One of the longest shots, hedge-fund billionaire and Mike Bloomberg wannabe Whitney Tilson (b. 1966), sought to make his name by outflanking Cuomo to the right. Tilson, who looks like Steve Martin's classic character in *The Jerk*, was a first-time candidate best known for helping found Teach for America, an anti-union initiative. Strangely, when he and Cuomo started attacking Mamdani's for his lack of experience, nobody asked the deep-pocketed novice pol why he was qualified to run City Hall.

In the run-up to the Wednesday debate, Tilson's campaign released a scattershot attack on Zohran. Inflammatorily titled "Socialists at the Gate," a fifteen-second spot posted on YouTube and other platforms showed a montage of clips of the DSA insurgent, including when Zohran angrily confronted MAGA border czar Tom Homan. Many Democrats familiar with Mamdani's show of force no doubt supported the direct action.

Like Cuomo, Tilson is not Jewish (although his wife is), but the New England WASP is also incensed by Mamdani's criticisms of Israel. With "antisemitism" written across the screen, the narrator of "Socialists at the Gate" warns that the leftists "demand consequences for genocidal Zionist imperialism." The assumption here is that viewers would be alarmed by such a position—but the phrasing simply reinforced the pro-Palestine contention that Israel is, in fact, committing genocide.

Run Zohran Run!

Tilson's hit piece further assumes that Zohran and company's call to "abolish capitalism" would shock audiences and thus required no explanation. In this respect, Whitney shares the blinders of Bloomberg, Bill Ackman and their ilk. Capitalism obviously has been very good to the 1%. Why on earth would anyone oppose it?

*

Zohran rolled up to the Wednesday night debate at 30 Rock in high style. A marching band played a Mardi Gras Dixieland rendition of Woody Guthrie's anthem, "This Land Is Your Land," a staple at Bernie's presidential campaign events. A rag-tag group of cheerful volunteers held posters reading "Freeze the Rent," "Childcare for All," and the familiar "Zohran for NYC." The upbeat candidate seemed relaxed but ready.

When the debate kicked off, it was instantly clear that Zohran's run had fundamentally changed the focus of the election. Rather than Israel-Palestine, WNBC-TV politics reporter Melissa Russo explained, "We're going to begin tonight with the issue that polls show is number one for New Yorkers: affordability." After a brief rundown of how city residents feel "squeezed," Russo then asked candidates to present their "one big idea" that could help address the crisis "now."

What ensued was mind-boggling. Although Zohran's turn at the plate came seventh (among the nine candidates in the studio), the first six batters whiffed. Despite several decades of combined experience on debate stages, and two reminders from Russo that the question asked for an immediate cost-of-living remedy, each of the first five contenders launched into an opening statement focused mainly on their bios and long-range goals.

Before batter number six, Whitney Tilson, took his turn, Telemundo New York moderator Rosarina Bretón again stressed that the question is what candidates would do "NOW" about affordability.

"'Now' may take another two years," declared the cartoonish billionaire. Rather the "freeze the rent," the hedge-funder claimed he would "drop rents by 20% by unleashing the private sector" to produce two million units of new housing (a process that would take much longer than two years). Incredibly, none of the first six candidates coherently responded to a simple question.

The energetic "rookie" stepped to the plate, thanked the hosts, then stated the following:

> We are live here [at 30 Rock] in the most expensive city in the United States of America. One in four New Yorkers are living in poverty. And I am running to be your next mayor to make this city affordable. I will do so by freezing the rent for more than two million rent-stabilized tenants; by making the slowest buses in the country fast and free; and by delivering universal childcare. And I will pay for this by taxing the 1%—the billionaires and profitable corporations that Mr. Cuomo cares about more than working-class New Yorkers. I will ask them to pay their share, so that we can have a city that everyone can afford.

Run Zohran Run!

Zohran capped off the second part of his final sentence with a smile. It would be hard to script a more cogent response or surpass his polished delivery. From the jump, Mamdani told debate viewers the same thing that his thousands of canvassers did when they knocked at voters' doors. New Yorkers could now see for themselves that the up-and-comer believed in his own message.

Moreover, while presenting himself as an advocate for the 99%, Zohran also put Cuomo in a bind: How could the governor supported by Bloomberg and DoorDash deny that the 1% owned him?

It would be an exaggeration to claim that Zohran "won" the debate based on his first response, but it is easy to see how voters of all ages and backgrounds might embrace the likable young contender. New York has always had plenty of bullies, including one currently in the White House and a fellow Baby Boomer who grimaced on stage while a millennial insurgent stuck it to him.

Zohran was by no means the only candidate who ripped into Cuomo during the debate. Longshot Michael Blake, a former assemblyman from the Bronx, made headlines by calling the accused sexual harasser of being the "greatest threat to public safety." City Council speaker Adrienne Adams charged Cuomo with "slow-walking" Covid safety protections to minority communities during the pandemic. Brad Lander accused the frontrunner of lying.

The TV ratings showed a large upswing from four years earlier. Over 725,000 viewers tuned in. Regardless of whether that was to see the rising star or a familiar face, the numbers favored Zohran. He needed more voters to turn out, whereas Cuomo sought less.

*

Perhaps more important than the back-and-forth in the debate itself is how various media outlets presented the highlights. It's quite likely that a large majority of viewers did not hang in for the full two hours (with the first half televised before it switched over to the internet). Whether or not they caught it live, prospective voters digested news clips the next day that helped shape their views of the race.

Even rival campaigns surely would be forced to admit that Zohran fared surprisingly well in local TV news reports. The audiences for such programs are generally older, and the few reporters Cuomo trusts are fixtures on city television stations. Intentionally or not, many of those same newscasts ended up giving lots of positive coverage to Mamdani. When a candidate is the center of controversy, news teams pay close attention.

On Thursday morning, June 4, NY1's popular morning host Pat Kiernan played a set of clips that started with Zohran questioning Cuomo's funding from billionaires.[79] On WABC TV, which has the largest local viewership, the highlights began with the Queens assemblyman declaring that his "biggest mistake" was "trusting Cuomo," who cut Medicaid funding during the pandemic. FOX5's sequence

---

79 Segments are also looped repeatedly on the cable network.

opened with the frontrunner incurring fire from Mamdani, Blake, Adrienne Adams, and Lander.

Most of the news segments included a Cuomo jibe against Mamdani. In one of his viral statements that night, Zohran insisted that he was "Trump's worst nightmare—a progressive Muslim immigrant who actually fights for the things that I believe in." Cuomo shot back that "Donald Trump would go through Mr. Mamdami [sic] like a hot knife through butter." Prior to Cuomo's usage, the metaphor had recently appeared twice in *Forbes*.

Even when he scored points, Mario's son seemed like he was living in a different era, griping about Zohran's use of "Twitter." More unexpected was that after leaving office amid two scandals nearly four years earlier, Cuomo's responses to any questions about nursing homes during the pandemic or the harassment allegations lacked punch.

Given the firestorm of criticism Zohran faced over the preceding three weeks regarding Israel-Palestine, it seemed certain that the issue would come up sooner than the tail end of the second hour. But the exchanges still provided plenty of tabloid fodder. Unlike Cuomo, Tilson, Adrienne Adams, and Scott Stringer, Mamdani said that his first trip as mayor would not be to Israel. Instead, he would stay home and "confront antisemitism directly."

Next asked whether Israel has the "right to exist," Zohran replied "Yes, as a state with equal rights for anyone." Cuomo and Tilson got pretty worked up about Mamdani's position.

In the eyes of the Baby Boomers standing to his right, Zohran's twin declarations were nothing short of political heresy. Tilson declared that in the unlikely event that he got elected mayor, he'd make his "fourth trip" to Israel, followed his "fifth trip to Ukraine."[80]

One month before the Fourth of July, the fireworks were already getting started.

---

80 Despite its importance to many Eastern European voters in the city, the Russia-Ukraine war rarely surfaced in the primary campaign.

CHAPTER 12

Five-Alarm Fire!

Immediately after the debate at 30 Rock, Zohran's team released major news: An endorsement from Alexandria Ocasio-Cortez. The congresswoman's backing for her fellow millennial DSA member representing northwest Queens[81] helped Mamdani move into the national spotlight.

After the *New York Times* first announced AOC's support, Zohran was all over the mainstream media. Leading national Democrats now paid close attention. On the night after the debate, MSNBC host Jen Psaki called Mamdani's campaign a "litmus test" for the party. The always on-message newcomer talked up his November 2024 outreach to Trump voters.

---

81 AOC's district spans from Astoria across the East River to the southeast Bronx (thus including Rikers Island). Zohran's assembly district covers Astoria and Long Island City.

Run Zohran Run!

AOC's plug for Zohran caused one of the candidates on stage at the Wednesday debate to humiliate herself. State Senator Jessica Ramos, who never gained traction in the race, had long feuded with AOC. Ramos' senate district, which covers Jackson Heights, Corona, East Elmhurst, is also the Congresswoman's turf.

After AOC came out for Zohran, Ramos tried to shank her rival but in the process became a laughingstock. The state senator suddenly opted to join the dozens of elected officials who had righteously called for Gov. Cuomo to resign in 2021 but now endorsed his 2025 bid for mayor because they thought he would win. Multiple platforms blew up with ridicule for Ramos.[82]

On Friday morning, the ever-so gracious Cuomo advised a very large throng of reporters at the Carpenters Union Hall that Ramos "is endorsing me. I am not endorsing her." AOC weighed in by posting "lol. lmao" above Cuomo's remark, a double-diss that seemed far more appropriate than repetitive.

Why there was so much coverage of the Ramos-Cuomo presser merits attention. As I noted on X at the time, this gossipy "story" was totally irrelevant. A candidate with miniscule poll numbers now backed the frontrunner out

---

82 While in the state senate since 2018, Ramos, a former union activist, had allied with the left. Shortly after Trump was elected, Ramos insisted that she had "always been to the right of the left," a craven move (and the opposite of Zohran's response to the Dems' defeat).

of spite. How could this possibly affect the outcome of the primary?

Alas, in-fighting and backbiting can yield clicks.

*

Someone else was hungry for attention that Friday morning in Downtown Manhattan. Last seen menacing Zohran and company five days earlier in Sunset Park, RR now showed up at a Mamdani campaign stop in the financial district. He was soon taken away in handcuffs.

As PIX11's website matter-of-factly explained, "The suspect confronted Mamdani at the event, accusing him of being insufficiently supportive of Israel and Jewish people, and allegedly bit [a] volunteer when she intervened."

It's not clear whether RR, who is 55 and often wears a Puerto Rican flag, is Jewish. But like Cuomo, Whitney Tilson, and many of the key figures at the *New York Post*, he fashions himself as a ferocious opponent of antisemitism. Or perhaps he just really disdains Muslim candidates. RR's rage against Zohran caused him to chomp on the forearm of a young female housing activist, which led the Manhattan DA office to charge him with misdemeanor assault. Media coverage of the sickening incident was scant, presumably because most local reporters were attending Jessica Ramos' major announcement.

Throughout June 6, Zohran sported an aqua blue kurta in honor of Eid-al-Adha, one of the two most important Islamic holidays. Since 2015, local public schools have closed for two Eid celebrations, illustrating the growing presence of Muslims in New York City. On Friday evening, Mamdani landed at a different faith's house of worship.

"This is the first Eid I've spent in a church," quipped Lina Khan, the antimonopoly activist. Zephyr Teachout, Cuomo's 2014 Democratic challenger who is closely allied with Khan, also sat on the panel held at the Church of the Village on W. 13th Street.

As the three figures began discussing bans on junk fees and ending noncompete agreements, a pro-Palestine activist stood up and raised the "Israel's right to exist" question. "May all normalizers burn in hell!" shouted the female protester as she was escorted out. The panelists then offered criticisms of billionaires, monopolies, and Cuomo.

As captured on video by *Semafor*'s Dave Weigel, a second female demonstrator, clad in a hijab, soon jumped up and angrily repeated the criticism of the first activist, but also questioned whether Mamdani's recognition of Israel betrayed his faith. After reiterating his position on the obligations of international law, Zohran added, "the question of whether I'm a good Muslim is a step too far." It was a memorable Eid for both Mamdani and Khan.

Although the attacks on Zohran's position on Israel-Palestine overwhelmingly came from the political establishment, the DSA insurgent continued to incur fire from the radical left. In the not-distant future, the activist-turned-pol surely will square off with his former comrades, as well as the next generation of protest leaders that he is currently inspiring. It will be interesting to watch.

*

Theodore Hamm

On the same Friday morning, Zohran went on HOT 97's *Ebro in the Morning*, a popular FM-radio show that streams across multiple platforms. The program appeals to fans of hip-hop culture, providing the former Mr. Cardamom with a chance to explain his ideas to a cross-section of Black and Latino listeners.

Ebro Darden (b. 1975 and raised in the Bay Area, where he attended Hebrew school) began the extended conversation by asking Zohran how he would pay for the key items on his agenda. Previewing a post-primary dust-up, the socialist candidate explained that rapper 50 Cent "is not going to be happy" about Mamdani's plan to tax the rich. Ebro seemed on-board, however.

The host allowed the fast-rising pol to thoroughly refute the "higher taxes will make rich people leave the city" line thrown around by the 1% and their minions. As the guest explained, the numbers show the opposite: it is working-class people who are leaving the increasingly unaffordable city. Ebro summed up his guest's position as "rich people are full of shit." "You said it," Zohran laughingly replied, "but that's the accurate conclusion."

The show's Latina co-host Laura Stylez then opened the door for Zohran to discuss his plan to open city-run grocery stores in "food deserts," with the candidate explaining the problems faced by residents of Queensbridge Houses, the massive public housing complex in Mamdani's assembly district. And after Zohran explained what he referred to as his "universalist" position on Palestinian equal rights, co-host Peter Rosenberg averred that "I'm sure you have a lot of support from the progressive Jewish community."

Run Zohran Run!

In the aftermath of the first debate, mainstream news outlets continued to attack Mamdani regarding Israel as well as the cost of his policy proposals. The short format of most contemporary political news stories typically allows for only a brief comment or two from a candidate explaining an issue. And hit pieces are not intended to foster discussion.

Ebro and company thus gave Zohran the chance to inform listeners about the actual details of his positions. Three weeks later, *Documented NY* reporter Prajwal Bhat mentioned that a Turkish immigrant named Erhan Tuncel was listening attentively to the interview while driving a taxi. It's hard to directly calculate the impact of any single interview on voter turnout—but HOT 97's hip-hop crowd clearly showed up for Mamdani.

Ebro was neither the first nor the biggest urban media figurehead to take interest in Zohran. Dominican American Kid Mero (b. 1983)—who frequently partners with Jamaican American Desus Nice (b. 1981) as a comic duo best known as the Bodega Boys—hails from the Bronx (as does Nice). When Mero first sat down with Zohran in late April, the host began by calling Cuomo a "disgraced bozo," setting the table for the newcomer to win over the Kid's fans.

In the final ten days of the primary race, Mero would play a high-profile role in the campaign. But a low-key figure with a massive audience gave Zohran an even stronger push. South Carolina-raised Charlamagne Tha God (b. 1978) is the main co-host of *The Breakfast Club*, a nationally syndicated radio program with at least 4.5 million listeners. The show also has comparable numbers of enthusiasts on Instagram and TikTok.

Although Charlamagne over the past decade has been a frequent critic of the Democratic Party establishment, he has not supported Bernie, arguing that the senator's 2020 presidential agenda did not directly address the concerns of Black voters. However, on Wednesday morning, June 11, the host clearly was impressed by Zohran.

"I love that idea," Charlamagne responded after the newcomer explained his proposal to send teams of trained outreach workers to help people experiencing episodes of emotional distress on the subway and elsewhere. A leading proponent of mental health awareness, Charlamagne relayed the clip to his 4.5 million followers on Instagram. In the comments section, a post that "this guy may be making too much sense for a politician" got 200 likes in the first six hours.

Charlamagne further observed that "anybody who is going to be the future of the Democratic Party [must] throw that old regime under the bus." That means "Not just Cuomo, but Schumer" and company, the host continued. "Trust me, I hear you," Zohran replied. "Because I have been critical of the style of leadership that gave rise to Donald Trump."

When the primary results came in two weeks later, Zohran's numbers showed strong gains among all voters categorized as millennials, meaning ages 25 to 39. As leftist Substacker Josh Ettinger observed on X, along with South Asians, Black people in that bracket came out in droves. The *Breakfast Club* appearance was by no means the only reason why Zohran racked up large numbers of young PoC votes, but the show certainly helped boost the insurgent's momentum.

Charlamagne may not be an actual god, but Zohran's vote totals in Harlem and Central Brooklyn suggest that the hip-hop figurehead strongly influences mortals.

*

Zohran and his team found a slot in his packed daily schedule in early June for the candidate to return to Staten Island. This time it was to illustrate that his key platform proposal regarding free buses had a clear precedent: the no-cost ferry that brings residents back and forth from their island to the slightly more famous one.

By this point, everything Zohran posted garnered lots of attention on social media. Even though the ferry video lacked gimmicks, it got plenty of traction. Perhaps even more important was the favorable coverage the candidate's trip received in the *Staten Island Advance*, the borough's longstanding "hometown" outlet. Older residents of the oft-neglected borough no doubt appreciated a visit from the celebrity newcomer.

Cuomo and his sputtering campaign may not have won over many new voters, but Michael Bloomberg got on board. Zohran's momentum caused Bloomy (as the *New York Post* often called him) to make a last-ditch effort to boost the guy who had been so friendly to luxury condo developers as governor. Mere mention of the word socialism is deeply unsettling for the former mayor.

In the 2020 Democratic campaign, Bloomberg spent over $1.1 billion of his own money in order to help party leaders sink Bernie. The DNC even changed its own rules regarding the required number of donors so that Bloomy could participate in a debate (in which Elizabeth Warren memorably slammed him). The former New York City mayor won very few delegates but somehow prevailed in the American Samoa caucus.

While there was no "perfect choice" in the race, and Bloomberg acknowledged that Cuomo was a difficult figure to work with, the billionaire praised the former governor's work in renovating La Guardia Airport. Bloomy sounded a bit gloomy about his choice. Over the next week, he nonetheless pumped $8.5 million into Fix the City's grimy efforts against Zohran.

Bloomberg's endorsement allowed Zohran's campaign to amplify its recurring line of attack on the increasingly vulnerable frontrunner. "Billionaires are consolidating around Andrew Cuomo because they know he will preserve the broken status quo," declared Team Mamdani.

Elsewhere in Midtown, the *New York Times* tried to wield its influence, but the organization was still recovering from a self-inflicted gunshot wound. In the summer of 2024, the *Times* made an odd decision, opting to no longer endorse candidates in local elections. Few organizations voluntarily surrender their own power, but in the outlet's own coverage of the decision, opinion editor Kathleen Kingsbury offered no clear explanation for it.

Four years earlier, the *Times* editorial board strongly backed novice pol Kathryn Garcia, who almost defeated Eric Adams. The paper's endorsement was also a leading reason why Alvin Bragg prevailed over a very well-heeled opponent in the race for Manhattan district attorney that year.

As the 2025 primary took shape, there were rumors that Kingsbury and company were rethinking their decision. Word traveled that the *Times* was consulting the city's leading lights for guidance.

On the morning of June 12, the Gray Lady—as the *Times* was often called in the twentieth century, referring to the paper's somber, anti-sensational tone—rolled out what turned out be its first big editorial statement about the race. Seven of the fifteen "experts" consulted by the Lady had selected Brad Lander as the best candidate for mayor. Mamdani was tied for second, with two votes, the same number as Cuomo and Tilson (!).

Like the *Times* target readership, the panelists skewed from professional middle class to the city elite. Although roughly 20% of the city's workforce is unionized, only one member claimed a labor affiliation in their bio. The president of the far-right Manhattan Institute joined Mike Bloomberg's deputy in backing billionaire Tilson. The co-founder of Warby Parker eyewear saw good things in Cuomo, and restaurateur Danny Meyer hungered for a Lander administration.

Victor Ng, an Asian graphic designer and Brooklyn political activist, and longtime Bronx Black community organizer Mychal Johnson provided Zohran's two votes. Although the *Times* released the expert panel's findings in order to give Lander a boost at that night's debate, the roundabout plug was not the same as a full declaration of support from the influential outlet.

While the *New York Post* editorial board is always hyper-aggressive, ready to smash a beer glass on your head, the *Times* here was needlessly passive-aggressive, essentially saying "we're not thrilled with Lander but several people we respect like him."

Bloomy and the *Times* would soon link arms in their fight against Zohran, with unexpected results.

*

CUNY's John Jay College of Criminal Justice hosted the second and final televised debate on Thursday night, June 12. NY1 was the lead sponsor. *Inside City Hall*'s Errol Louis, WNYC's mainstay Brian Lehrer, and *The City*'s Katie Honan moderated.

This time the seven leading contenders (thus excluding Jessica Ramos and Michael Blake) on stage began with 60-second opening statements. Batting third, Tilson quickly segued from presenting his bio to attacking Zohran. With his fingers randomly pointing in different directions, the ultra-rich dude declared that "we need a mayor who is experienced, competent and can get things done—not a social media phenom with cute videos." Tilson was clearly on track to get more than 450,000 fewer 1st-place votes than Mamdani.

Up sixth, Zohran again started strong, energetically invoking affordability, taxing the rich, Trump, Cuomo's funding from right-wing billionaires, authoritarianism, his own immigrant experience, the need for "a new generation of leadership," and his grassroots momentum. He then cheerfully invited viewers to "join us—and let's win a New York you can afford." Cuomo followed with a downbeat emphasis on "management" and "experience."

All week, the unnerved frontrunner had been repetitively attacking Zohran's because the insurgent's resume listed no executive positions. Cuomo summoned his preferred local TV reporters, including WCBS shotcaller Marcia Kramer and WABC veteran N.J. Burkett, to an empty pocket park somewhere in Midtown East (the former governor's version of a "Rose Garden.") As he belittled his youthful rival, Cuomo called his big backer Bloomberg the "last great manager-mayor" of the city.

When Errol Louis raised the age question, he included a twist, pointing out that if elected, Zohran would be the youngest New York City mayor in over a century, but Cuomo would be the oldest. The 33-year-old came to the debate with a ready response. "Judge me by the campaign I am running," Zohran declared. "A campaign that we began with about two full-time employees, polling at one percent, [has] now grown to be one in which we manage over 36,000 volunteers that have knocked on nearly a million doors."

When Louis then asked Cuomo whether his advancing age might raise any concerns, the 67-year-old fired off a bunch of talking points about Mamdani's lack of accomplishments. While the non-answer did not make the frontrunner look good, it also opened the door for the insurgent—whose name the veteran Democrat again mispronounced—to fire back. Virality ensued.

In a clip seen worldwide, Zohran confidently stated:

> *To Mr. Cuomo: I have never had to resign in disgrace. I have never cut Medicaid.* [Loud cheers from debate audience.] *I have never stolen hundreds of millions of dollars from the MTA. I have never hounded the thirteen women who credibly accused me of sexual harassment. I have never sued for their gynecological records. And I have never done those things because I am not you, Mr. Cuomo. And furthermore, the name is Mamdani: M-A-M-D-A-N-I.* [Raucous cheers.] *You should learn how to say it, because we gotta get it right.*

As the young title contender pounded away for thirty seconds, the split-screen showed Goliath looking down the entire time, fuming. The bigoted bully responded by once more mispronouncing Mamdani, causing Zohran to correct him yet again.

Hasan Piker and the rest of the internet went nuts. The debate was effectively over, and in retrospect, so was the primary.

Run Zohran Run!

"When we simulated the second debate a few days beforehand," noted Andrew Epstein. "I played Cuomo's part. I needled Zohran quite a bit, consistently botching his name." Andrew says that deputy communications director Lekha Sunder suggested the needling during the rehearsal, accurately predicting that it would inspire Zohran to fight back.

At John Jay that Thursday night in June, Mamdani summoned the spirit of Muhammad Ali, who famously demanded that a rival in the ring say his name.

*

Two nights later, the theater of action was just two blocks away from John Jay. Terminal 5, a 3,000-capacity concert venue, was a hot ticket that night. Once the "warm-up act to the warm-up act" in Kampala, Zohran was now a Manhattan headliner. AOC, a.k.a. Jessica Ramos' archrival, shared the bill.

Kid Mero hosted. Mamdani's campaign events coordinator Katie Riley handled logistics and Julian Gerson assembled an impressive undercard. There was John Samuelsen, the transit workers leader who had once been close allies with Cuomo, John Liu, and Maf Misbah Udin, the Bangladeshi president of the national Alliance of South Asian-American Labor. The DSA's Alexa Avilés and Claire Valdez also stepped up to the microphone.

After Mero warmed up the mostly twenty-something crowd, the fifty-something Samuelsen touted Zohran's plan for free buses in his distinctive Brooklyn accent.

Next came Avilés, a Boricua contemporary of Samuelsen who also speaks in an old-school way. "That's right, boo," the councilwoman said repeatedly, as the crowd joined her in deriding Mayor Adams, Cuomo, and their billionaire backers.

When Avilés declared that Israel hawks were targeting her because of her support for a "free Palestine," the polyglot entourage of Mamdani supporters on stage wildly cheered, and the next-gen audience went nuts. It was a beautiful sight to behold.

A city led by working people expressing global solidarity is not what Mike Bloomberg, the *New York Times* and the *New York Post* envision. But that's the way the cookie crumbled.

PART THREE:
TRIUMPH

CHAPTER 13
The Spoils of Victory

"We need a 'big swing,'" Zohran advised his inner circle as primary day neared. Invoking a malleable term used in public policy circles, the candidate here referred to a spectacle that captured the essence of his campaign. Amid the topsy-turvy final week of the primary, Mamdani and his team brainstormed ideas.

Julian Gerson, then Zohran's political director (now speechwriter), proposed that the magnetic figure walk from the top of Manhattan to the bottom. As Julian explained to other members of the candidate's inner circle, a "march" would help Zohran invoke Mahmood Mamdani's participation in SNCC protests in the mid-1960s. Moreover, the younger Mamdani "radiates hope and joy in a joyless time—so getting him out there to interact with as many different people as possible seemed like the right move," Gerson later told me.

Run Zohran Run!

After Zohran supported Julian's proposal, the planning began, with Elle Bisgaard-Church handling logistics like security and staffing, and deputy campaign manager Katie Riley plotting the route. The weather looked good for the evening of June 20, the first night of summer and the final Friday before the primary. And things worked out rather well. This big swing produced a home run *and* a sixer.

With Julian and top aide Spencer Goldberg at his side for the distance, Zohran—clad in a white business shirt with a black tie, black pants, and gray sneakers—got numerous dabs, shoulder bumps, thumbs ups, and peace signs from folks uptown. As the candidate-led entourage traversed down Broadway through the Upper West Side, young women hopped and clapped at the sight of Mamdani. Middle-aged men squealed.[83]

Under the bright lights at Times Square, a hip-hop workout entourage—mostly likely fans of Charlamagne, *Ebro in the Morning*, and/or Kid Mero and his sidekick Desus—took selfies with a beaming Zohran.[84] Young Black and brown dudes showing love for a socialist in the city's most iconic location wasn't exactly what Mike Bloomberg and his crowd wanted to see. Neither did the media powerhouse that gave rise to the name of Times Square.

---

83 As *Gothamist*'s Elizabeth Kim stated on X that night, "The democratic socialist candidate for mayor walking down Park Ave [i.e. Bloomberg's Upper East Side turf] would sure be a photo for the ages."

84 In mid-July, Jamaal Bowman brought Zohran to a Wu-Tang Clan show at Madison Square Garden. Mamdani then posted a video showing the candidate receiving a friendly reception from both fellow concertgoers and Wu-Tang figurehead RZA (b. 1969).

As Zohran zigzagged through the East Village after midnight, twenty-somethings poured out of bars to catch a glimpse of a potential future mayor not much older than them. One burly lad who clearly appeared to enjoy his suds whooped deliriously after shaking the rock star's hand. The would-be mayor soon posed for a picture beside the statue of a clapping Fiorello La Guardia near NYU.

Within a month, the Mamdani campaign's three-minute sizzle reel of the event—with campaign videographer Donald Borenstein directing a crew and Olivia Becker editing copious footage—surpassed 15 million views on the Musk platform. A 19-second TikTok clip that showed Mira Nair hugging Zohran along the route, expressing concern that her son had been "eating unhealthy things," clocked over 2.3 million looks.

A walk from Inwood Hill Park at the northern end of Manhattan to Battery Park at the southern tip is 12.5 miles and typically takes nearly five hours. Detours add mileage. If you're shaking hands and taking countless selfies with fans, the clock extends. Zohran and company reached the Staten Island ferry terminal in Battery Park at 2:15 a.m., over eight hours after Mamdani's Manhattan waltz began.

Along with roughly three dozen youthful supporters, Mamdani posed for a cheerful group pic. According to *Hell Gate*'s Max Rivlin-Nadler, the candidate then chatted with his enthusiasts for about half an hour before departing.

"I'm exhausted but I'm living off the adrenaline of it," Zohran told Max the end of the night. "We're right where we want to be." Primary day was just over 72 hours away.

Run Zohran Run!

Rather than take a free ride on the 24-hour ferry to Staten Island, Zohran went home to Astoria. As noted by Rivlin-Nader, the candidate needed to get some rest before returning to Harlem in order to address Rev. Al Sharpton's Saturday morning meeting. There, after explaining why his middle name is Kwame, Zohran informed a receptive audience that Mahmood Mamdani "marched with SNCC." Although he did not mention his tour through Harlem the previous night, at least a few folks in the audience likely knew about it.

On Monday, GoodPoliticGuy (GPC), a DC-based socialist YouTube commentator, quote-tweeted Zohran's release of the Friday night walk video. Referring to a Mamdani victory the next day, GPC spoke for many on the left across the globe when he stated, "I know nothing good ever happens but please god can we have just this one."

*

"Friday is a blessed day," Brooklynite Asad Dandia tweeted on the morning of Zohran's Manhattan march. Noting that the candidate and his team had reached out to over 130 mosques,[85] Asad included a picture of himself embracing Zohran, then wrote, "I'm Sunni, you're Shia, so we've got our bases covered" with a laughing emoji.[86]

---

85 Mohamed Alharbi handled the campaign's outreach to Muslim and South Asian communities. Raised in a Yemeni household in the Bronx, Alharbi is in his mid-twenties.

86 At the June 12 debate, Errol Louis asked Cuomo if he had ever visited a mosque while a statewide elected official. "I believe I have," the veteran Democrat replied, without citing an example.

Born in 1992 at Coney Island Hospital, Asad grew up in a Sunni household in Brighton Beach with family roots in Pakistan. Like Bernie Sanders and Chuck Schumer, Asad graduated from James Madison High School in Midwood, Brooklyn. During Mayor Bloomberg's final year in office, Dandia was a lead plaintiff in *Raza v. City of New York*, a landmark ACLU case that helped curtail NYPD surveillance of Muslim communities.

Zohran and Asad, now a New York City historian and tour guide, became pals in August 2024, when the assemblyman reached out to the Brooklyn activist to discuss his potential run for mayor. When they first met in person at Café Reggio in the West Village, Asad wore a T-shirt featuring the familiar Greek NYC coffee cup accompanied by a bacon, egg, and cheese on a roll.

The shirt prompted Zohran to jokingly quiz his fellow Muslim about his diet. "Don't worry, it's turkey bacon," Asad assured him. The two became fast friends.

At the end of the fall 2021 hunger strike that Zohran had joined with taxi workers, the future mayoral candidate noted that he usually ended his ritual fasting by first eating a date. I asked Asad about the relationship between this Ramadan practice and Zohran's politics.

"We do so in the spirit of sacrifice," Asad explained. "We give up food and sex and resist other urges in the name of helping others." Like running marathons, fasting also requires incredible amounts of self-discipline.

Run Zohran Run!

When I first interviewed Zohran in late March, he told me that he looked forward to Jummah, the early Friday afternoon prayer congregations at mosques that the aspiring city leader joined regularly during the primary. "It's a brief moment of respite from the world," Mamdani explained. "In the midst of a campaign stop, that moment of losing oneself into a larger collective provides beauty for just a few minutes." There would be plenty of noise late in the race, heightening the importance of any quietude the candidate could find.

As a distance runner and a practicing Muslim, Zohran can tap into a vast reservoir of self-regenerating energy. People who worked closely with him during the primary remain awestruck by his stamina.

Andrew Epstein said Zohran's daytime fuel is most frequently derived from peanut butter and banana smoothies. Mamdani drinks chai in the morning and iced coffee later in the day, albeit not regularly, and plenty of water. At night he consumes lots of different food, preferably Indian. One of the few positive stories in the *New York Times* about Zohran mentioned that Mira Nair once cooked biryani with chicken for her son and campaign staffers.

Shortly after Zohran's upset win, MAGA influencers on the Musk site including Laura Loomer, Charlie Kirk, and @endwokeness posted a clip of a 2023 interview in which Mamdani ate a halal platter of chicken and rice with his hands. The practice is common throughout South Asia, Africa and many parts of the world, but its "foreignness" was too much for the Trump crowd. "Civilized people in America don't eat like this," declared a next-gen far-right

Texas Congressman, demanding that Zohran "adopt Western customs or go back to the Third World."

In the wake of Mamdani's primary victory, Rep. Marjorie Taylor Greene, the MAGA congresswoman from Georgia, circulated an image of the Statue of Liberty wearing a burqa. Tucker Carlson called Zohran a "foreign-born nitwit." MAGA strategist Steve Bannon, a far-right populist, sought to understand why a far-left populist succeeded in the June election. "This guy is a very skilled politician," Bannon told *Meet the Press* host Kristen Welker. "He's got radical ideas, but he presents them in a sunny upbeat way and people feel like he's fighting for them, particularly on an issue that Republicans haven't connected on yet: affordability."[87]

Meanwhile, Trump pushed through a deeply regressive tax cut that rewards the 1%.

*

Mamdani's homestretch run was full of highs, including a Working Families Party rally in Crown Heights on Sunday night, June 22. The event was hosted by Tish James and Chi Ossé, with appearances from Jabari Brisport, Justin Brannan, and a slew of mayoral candidates opposing Cuomo. "Zohran has sparked a level of enthusiasm that I have not seen since the days of 'change,'" James declared, referring to Obama's ground-breaking 2008 campaign.

---

87 MTG, Carlson, and Bannon were impressed by Mamdani's ability to succeed while criticizing Israel. It appeared that the MAGA figureheads sought to win over Democrats angry with their party's deference to Netanyahu.

Run Zohran Run!

But the last week also brought plenty of lows. On Tuesday, June 17, the insurgent did a streamed podcast with *The Bulwark*, a Never-Trump outlet. Near the end of the one-hour conversation, host Tim Miller (b. 1981), a former Jeb Bush operative, brought up Israel, Palestine, and antisemitism.

"'Globalize the intifada' is a very popular phrase at protests on the left," Miller asserted. "Maybe some people are saying that with good intent, but there are certainly some people who are saying that phrase with violent intent." The host did not offer specific examples of the phrase instigating violence against Jewish people. But Zohran's response provided his pro-Israel foes with a weapon they would deploy ceaselessly for the next several weeks.

Rather than offer the blistering denunciation that his critics demanded, Zohran committed what has become a thought crime in Trump's America. Rather than a kneejerk reaction, Mamdani offered context and nuance. The candidate first referred to the "horrific war crime of October 7," then provided anecdotes he had heard from Jewish city residents about the fear they felt in the aftermath.

Although Zohran further mentioned his campaign's proposal to greatly expand anti-hate crime programming, the host remained focused on activist slogans, prompting this exchange:

> Mamdani: *I am someone less comfortable with the idea of banning the use of certain words— and I think it is more evocative of a Trump-style approach to how to lead a country.*

Miller: *Sure, but does the phrase globalizing the intifada make you uncomfortable?*

Mamdani: *I know people for whom the phrase means very different things. And to me, ultimately, what I hear from so many people is a desperate desire for equality and equal rights in standing up for Palestinian human rights. And I think what's difficult also is that the very word has been used by the Holocaust Museum when translating the Warsaw ghetto uprising into Arabic because it's a word that means struggle. And as a Muslim man who grew up post-9/11, I'm all too familiar with the way in which Arabic words can be twisted, distorted, and used to justify any kind of meaning. And I think that's where it leaves me with a sense that what we need to do is focus on keeping Jewish New Yorkers safe.*[88]

Prominent voices on the left applauded Zohran's thoughtful response. Brooklyn College professor Corey Robin called it "a model of integrity—not sacrificing one's values or pandering to voters—while demonstrating sensitivity to those voters and their concerns." Nerdeen Kiswani, the founder of Within Our Lifetime who previously slammed the candidate's position on Israel's "right to exist," now praised Mamdani's resolve.

But thoughtful responses are a distinct exception in the era of soundbite discourse. Thunderous condemnation of

---

[88] Note: Edited for clarity. See https://podscripts.co/podcasts/the-bulwark-podcast/zohran-mamdani-fypod-crossover.

Run Zohran Run!

Zohran's often-distorted comments reverberated well into July, egged on by Andrew Cuomo, Rep. Hakeem Jeffries, the CEO of Pfizer, and anyone seeking to burst the socialist candidate's bubble. After a torrential month-long downpour, the Democratic mayoral nominee told the Big Pharma guy and his crowd that he would "discourage others" from using a phrase that Mamdani had never stated.

From late October through the middle of June, Zohran and his team made almost no significant tactical mistakes. Opening the door to the Never-Trump crowd carried more risks than rewards, however. It's not clear how the old-guard Republican audience could yield votes in a New York City primary contest in which voters needed to be registered Democrats.

One day before *The Bulwark* conversation, Mamdani chatted with *The Meidas Touch*, an extremely popular podcast that is certainly "anti-Trump" but—unlike *The Bulwark*—not aligned with the Bush wing of the Republicans. *Meidas* host Ben Meiselas is Colin Kaepernick's lawyer and business partner. That conversation was friendly, whereas Tim Miller clearly laid a trap, one that could have been avoided.

As Corey Robin pointed out, many of Mamdani's loudest critics, including Miller and Hakeem Jeffries, "are not Jewish but nevertheless like to speak on behalf of us and our alleged fears." In mid-July, the former governor (raised Catholic) told upscale congregants at a synagogue in the Hamptons he would "wager that a majority of Jews" voted for Zohran. Even though Cuomo claimed "most Jews voted for Mamdani," Peter Beinart observed on X, he still insisted that "Mamdani must be defeated in order to keep Jewish New Yorkers safe. Makes perfect sense."

As Beinart stated in his initial post-primary analysis, Zohran's victory showed that very large numbers of young voters in New York City were now pro-Palestine. As even pro-Israel analysts surely would concur, that is a monumental shift in U.S. politics. Meanwhile, many liberal Jews over 35 likely shared the perspective of Brad Lander, the third-place finisher whose supporters overwhelmingly ranked Mamdani second. Lander told CNN's Jake Tapper in late June that he and fellow Jewish voters objected to being used as "pawns" by Bibi's backers.

Tapper and many of his peers in the national media downplayed the bread-and-butter issues integral to Zohran's rise, instead keeping Israel at the center of their coverage of Mamdani's victory. Waleed Shahid, a Democratic strategist who worked for both AOC and Cynthia Nixon, conducted a revealing study that reviewed the first week of broadcast coverage after June 24.

Whether from a liberal (MSNBC), centrist (CNN), or conservative (Fox News) outlet, over 60% of national TV reports about Zohran foregrounded his positions on Israel-Palestine. Fox, of course, led the pack in Mamdani mentions, churning out 154 segments (nearly double the amount by the other two networks). Shahid found that 64% of those reports explicitly referred to Israel or antisemitism. "You've got Hamas sympathizers winning in NYC, and the media's silent about it," declared one Fox commentator, seemingly unaware of his own bluster.

Run Zohran Run!

New York City's local TV outlets placed more emphasis on Zohran's cost-of-living agenda. According to Shahid, these stations, including the Fox affiliate, nonetheless brought up Israel-related controversies in just over 40% of the segments.

At the Hamptons synagogue on July 20, Cuomo highlighted his "family tradition." "Like my father before me," the defeated primary candidate said, "I was the most aggressive governor in the United States on behalf of Israel." Blind loyalty is quite a dangerous tradition. Meanwhile, one of Eric Adams' two fall ballot lines is called "EndAntiSemitism."[89]

While the Boomer Dems pander to Israel's murderous regime, the party's growing ranks of young pro-Palestine voters advocate both peace and equality.

*

Soon after the "globalize the intifada" controversy exploded, Mamdani called attention to the violence he had faced in recent weeks. At an East Harlem sidewalk presser highlighting his endorsement from Maya Wiley, the progressive third-place finisher in the 2021 Democratic primary, the rising star became emotional. "I get threats on my life and on the people that I love, and I try not to talk about it because the function of racism, as Toni Morrison

---

89 The other is "Safe&Affordable." No spaces are permitted on ballot lines.

said, is distraction," Zohran said, fighting back tears. He then pivoted back to making the city affordable.[90]

While Mamdani walked the city streets, Cuomo preferred to sit at the wheel of his Dodge Charger. On Monday, June 16, *Daily News* reporter Josie Stratman posted a pic of the frontrunner's car parked in a left-turn lane in Midtown, a move known to further slow down already creeping traffic. The former governor had dropped by the hotel workers union headquarters to receive the group's backing, but his Charger antics got far more coverage than the 11th-hour endorsement.

Meanwhile, the escalating venom toward Zohran summoned darker sentiments shared by the city elite. Desperate for attention, Whitney Tilson—whose June polling numbers matched his 1% socioeconomic status—sought to whip up Islamophobic outrage. The billionaire donned a yarmulke and went to Brooklyn's Boro Park, home to many pro-Trump Orthodox Jews.

A 71-second video followed Tilson as he sought responses to the "globalize the intifada" controversy he helped stoke.[91] "I don't like what he said," an elderly man in a yarmulke said regarding Zohran's response to Tim Miller, adding that the insurgent candidate was a "danger." Things were starting to get pretty hot in that Boro Park bakery.

---

90 As MSNBC host Chris Hayes later noted, Zohran's ability to always stay on-message takes a page from the Bernie Sanders playbook.
91 The video included a clip of Tilson bringing up the phrase at the June 12 debate at John Jay College.

Run Zohran Run!

A middle-aged white guy who is not identifiably Jewish then informed the yarmulke-sporting WASP that Mamdani "looks like a dangerous person." Pouring gas into the proverbial dumpster, Tilson suggested to him that "you have to be looking around a little more" when people like Mamdani are nearby. It was not clear whether Whitney meant Zohran or all young Muslim men.

Tilson's attack belonged somewhere beneath the gutter. Like Vickie Paladino's call to "deport" Zohran, it should have been roundly denounced—instead, over the next month, *Jewish Daily Forward* reporter Jacob Kornbluh's X post debuting Tilson's ad was viewed nearly 300,000 times. In the age of Trump and Musk, hate travels quickly.

An even more incendiary anti-Zohran statement went live only a few minutes before Kornbluh rolled out Tilson's attack piece.[92] Ever since the Holocaust smears started in the middle of May, it seemed only a matter of time before a Mamdani opponent played the Hitler card. With four days to go, Elisha Wiesel, son of the famous Holocaust survivor and author Elie Wiesel, finally dealt it.

In a one-minute statement set to an ominous soundtrack, Elisha, a former chief information officer at Goldman Sachs, solemnly warns about where the election of a Muslim, pro-Palestine mayor would lead. Narrating while clips show Hitler at a microphone followed by Nazi flags, gunfire, and mass roundups, Elisha states that "rhetoric turned to violence—it metastasized into genocide."

---

92 Tilson posted the video on X three hours after Kornbluh.

When Wiesel refers to "new attacks on Jews," he first presents snippets of the October 7 Hamas kidnappings and incidents of antisemitic terror in U.S. cities—before adding footage of nonviolent pro-Palestine campus protests in New York City. A one-word banner reading "Intifada" drives home Elisha's far-right message: Any criticism of Israel is antisemitic.

Zohran first surfaces at the 20-second mark, with a clip of the mayoral candidate telling activists that he had co-founded Bowdoin College's chapter of Students for Justice in Palestine. Viewers next glimpse a news report stating that the group's New York State branches have "endorsed the use of violence and attacks against civilians." Wiesel does not bother to clarify that Bowdoin is in Maine.

The statement ends at Auschwitz, with a cameo from Oprah standing next to Elie Wiesel. "Talk to your friends, Jewish and non-Jewish," implores Elisha, "and ask them not to rank Zohran Mamdani—and to keep antisemitism off the ballot." Paid for by the Wiesel family, the hit piece ended with "#DoNotRankMamdani" across the screen. Over the next month, it garnered over 1.5 million views on X.

Two days after Tilson and Weisel stoked the fire, a small plane carrying a similar message circled Lower Manhattan, making it visible from Sunset Park. "Save NYC from Global Intifada. Reject Mamdani," the sky banner advised. Cuomo's irascible longtime spokesman helped call attention to it on the Musk platform.

Run Zohran Run!

This time the support came from a different set of ultra-nationalists. An outside spending group called Indian Americans for Cuomo paid $3,600 for the aerial statement. At the Public Theater forum in May, Zohran criticized India Prime Minister Narendra Modi, a Hindu nationalist. Akash Mehta, publisher of event co-sponsor *New York Focus*, asked candidates about India's ruler. Mamdani explained that his father's family hails from Gujarat, a large state northwest of Mumbai where Modi rose to power in the early 2000s.

At the candidate forum, Zohran told the audience that India's current prime minister "helped to orchestrate the mass slaughter of Gujurati Muslims." As a result, Mamdani stated, "We should view him in same manner as we do Benjamin Netanyahu—as a war criminal."

While his support for Netanyahu was quite evident, Cuomo had not said anything about Modi. The "Global Intifada" sky banner, meanwhile, only mentioned one candidate's name: Mamdani. Anyone from the "no publicity is bad publicity" school (from which Trump holds an honorary doctorate) can explain why the aerial attack did not hurt the insurgent.

*

Zohran's triumph on June 24 prompted a wave of death threats. According to a Council of American Islamic Relations-affiliated entity, there were over 125 hate-related reports involving the candidate or his campaign in just the first three days. At least 6,200 statements online during that same span contained an Islamophobic slur. Pro-Israel zealot Bill Ackman would soon play the 9/11 card, painting Zohran as pro-Al Qaeda because in 2004 Mahmood Mamdani argued that suicide bombers should be placed in the "category of soldier."

Mayor Adams responded to Cuomo's defeat by cozying up to Ackman and Daniel Loeb, who quickly cut ties to the primary's big loser. Ackman, who prefers not to play his cards close to the vest, wrote screeds on X detailing his search for a volunteer write-in candidate, which went nowhere. Ackman and Loeb thus settled on Adams, whom Loeb and other Israel hawks had pressured to bust up the pro-Palestine protests at Columbia the spring of 2024. The always-transactional mayor landed donations from the Bibi-loving billionaires.[93]

Adams invited Ackman and Loeb to choose key staff for his reelection bid. For campaign manager, the duo selected Eugene Noh, known in local politics for his no-holds-barred style. During the primary, Noh handled Whitney Tilson's field operation, which helped the bomb-throwing billionaire collect 8,500 votes, not a particularly good ROI for a campaign that spent over $3 million. Loeb and Ackman clearly know talent when they see it.

"We value their judgment very much, Dan and Bill," Adams' fixer Frank Carone told the *New York Times*. "These guys, they could be doing anything they want, but they're in the

---

93   As reported by the *Washington Post* (5-16-2024), shortly before the NYPD's violent raid on the Columbia campus, Adams participated in a Zoom call with Loeb, NYC developers Len Blavatnik and Joe Sitt, and Daniel Lubetzky, founder of Kind snack company.

Run Zohran Run!

trenches here worrying about the state of New York and understanding affordability is a big issue."

Fixers say the damnedest things. So, too, do the city's leading news outlets.

*

Just prior to the start of early voting on June 14, Hasan Piker, Medhi Hasan, and countless other influential commentators helped the "M-A-M-D-A-N-I" takedown of Cuomo at the June 12 debate blow up. Meanwhile, the *New York Times* brass was shook. One might even say that the handwriting was all over the internet. As they scrambled together a response over the weekend, the *Times* editorial team watched Zohran, AOC, and company rally their excited ranks. Populism of any variety unnerves the Gray Lady.

On Monday, June 16, the *Times* editorial board issued a statement for the ages. The mannerly title, "Our Advice to Voters in a Vexing Race for New York Mayor," evoked the first Gilded Age, before Manhattan became the power center of a five-borough city. The actual "advice" suited the second Gilded Age, when billionaires in Midtown skyscrapers control the unruly metropolis.

There is no doubt about which billionaire the *Times* most reveres. His cops may have visited terror on minority teenage males, and planted spies in mosques, but Mike Bloomberg understood the need for "effective management," or so the editorial team declared. This bunch clearly cherishes the e-word, using it five times in a not-long statement, including an evidence-free assertion that Whitney Tilson was "effectively running as Bloomberg's heir."[94]

Despite his very successful universal pre-K rollout, Bill de Blasio, according to the *Times*' finest minds, "set back the city's K-12 school system." The pro-Bloomberg set then declared that de Blasio's "main legacy is to have contributed to the city's recent decline." The insult would have been stinging if it rang true.

After grudging flattery about Zohran's "charisma" and "fresh political style," the *Times* team moved in for the kill. "Unfortunately, Mr. Mamdani is running on an agenda uniquely unsuited to the city's challenges," the board huffed. "He is a democratic socialist who too often ignores the unavoidable trade-offs of governance." The city surely did not need anything Zohran's platform offered. "We do not believe that Mr. Mamdani deserves a spot on New Yorkers' ballots," maintained the Gray Lady, a suggestion widely ignored.

It was quite disturbing, the *Times* said, that the 33-year-old candidate, who came-of-age during the Bloomberg era of stop and frisk and Muslim surveillance, had the nerve to call de Blasio the "best New York mayor of his lifetime." Even though they called for Cuomo's resignation in 2021, the editorial team now concluded that Mario's obnoxious

---

94 As seen earlier, Bloomberg's longtime operative Howard Wolfson was on the panel of fifteen "experts" and provided one of two first-place votes for Tilson. It's not clear if he was directly consulted for this statement, but his influence seems present.

kid really was the only option, citing Bloomberg's plug for the disgraced former governor as the main reason why.

In 21st-century parlance, the *Times* essentially said, "Cuomo sucks, but anything is better than Mamdani." Because the outlet's brass had voluntarily surrendered its endorsement power, the statement only "advised" voters to back the former governor. It did not mention Zohran's stance on Palestine—but, given the paper's clear bias for Israel, it's hard to ignore that as a leading reason for the *Times*' animus.[95]

The bombast backfired, producing yet another self-inflicted wound for the *Times*. A tsunami of derision flooded multiple platforms. Will Zohran's legions of young readers ever subscribe to a publication that hates what they stand for? The eleventh-hour plea for Cuomo was a "wimpy, disingenuous" move by the Gray Lady, de Blasio told *New York*'s Nia Prater. The former mayor added that if the attack on progressive politics "had come from the *New York Post*, I wouldn't have been surprised."

Rather than soften its stance towards the Democratic nominee, the *Times*' hostility towards Zohran after the primary mirrored the *Post*'s. First there was the aforementioned pseudo-scandal about Mamdani's Columbia application. At the end of July, the paper of record again stirred the pot.

---

95 See Adam Johnson's analysis of the *Times*' coverage of Gaza in *The Intercept* (1-9-2024).

In the wake of a mass shooting in Midtown Manhattan, the *Times* joined the *Post* and Andrew Cuomo in spotlighting the fact that Zohran was in Uganda at the time. "Mr. Mamdani's absence could hardly have been more poorly timed," asserted a story in the outlet's local section, thus suggesting that the candidate's ten-day trip to Uganda to celebrate his recent wedding was somehow a failure in leadership. When the Democratic nominee returned to town 36 hours after the incident, he was quickly embraced by family members of two of the Midtown murder victims.

Because the *Post* had spent the ten days beforehand cheering on Israel's strikes against Iran,[96] Mamdani did not return to the tabloid's cover until primary day. "Say It Ain't Zo!" warned the front page on June 24. A large sub-headline then brazenly stated, "The *POST* says: NYers must reject radical, antisemitic socialist in today's primary."

A full-page cover photo showed Zohran speaking at a 2021 rally, at which a female activist wearing a hijab stands next to him holding a Within Our Lifetime poster reading "There is only one solution: Intifada, Revolution." Beneath that young woman, a small box of text calls attention to the poster and falsely claims that Mamdani "still defends" use of the phrase "globalize the intifada." For the fast-dwindling number of *Post* fans who read the tabloid's print edition, the anti-Mamdani message was loud and clear.

That same morning, I chatted with Queens-based Ali Najmi, Zohran's election lawyer and a trailblazer in the

---

96 From June 13 through June 23, seven *Post* covers focused on Israel-Iran.

political advancement of New York City Muslims. We discussed the possibility of a defamation lawsuit against the *Post*. "Zohran has never said anything antisemitic," Ali said. But among other obstacles, the Murdoch machine has powerhouse lawyers who can make a legal battle very costly.[97]

The following day saw the "NYC SOS" cover, after which Zohran appeared frequently on the tabloid's front page, including four times during the first week after his victory. On July 5, a *Post* cover read "Uganda Be Joking," a weak pun that referred to the *New York Times*-hyped "scandal" regarding Mamdani's college application. The *Post* was happy to amplify a hit piece that seemed more suited for the Murdoch rag.

Two weeks later, when Zohran and his wife, graphic artist Rama Duwaji (b. 1998), traveled to Uganda for their wedding party, the candidate took a memorable swipe at the *Post*. In a short clip set to a generic contemporary African beat, Zohran stated that "since you will undoubtedly read about this trip in the *New York Post*"—adding "*Inshallah*, on the front page"—the candidate prepared some potential bad pun covers. Mock-ups showed lead headlines such as "M.I.A.? Mamdani In Africa," "Uganda Miss Me," and "He Afri-Can't Be Serious."

---

97 Even when a defamation plaintiff can establish that the defendant knowingly lied, establishing "harm" is often difficult. As Ali and I agreed on primary day, it looked like Zohran was en route to victory, so the *Post*'s smears would have no damaging impact.

Andrew Epstein, who in July changed his role in the campaign to become creative director, told me that he and Zohran scripted the much-shared video, with Andrew writing the spoof headlines. Graphic designer Debbie Saslaw, whose team at Melted Solids worked frequently with Zohran for NYC during the primary, composed the fake *Post* covers, which looked quite real. Donald Borenstein handled the shoot.

Rather than a lengthy defamation lawsuit, Mamdani and company fought back against the *Post* with clever ridicule. The tabloid responded by writing a story about Zohran's spoof. Amid its zealous pursuit of clicks, Murdoch's crew seemed punchdrunk.

*

In the middle of May, the DSA contender was consistently polling second, but still trailing Cuomo by 20 points. Even so, on May 15, *Indypendent* publisher and editor John Tarleton's story "Zohran Mamdani's Path to Victory" went live on its website. Six weeks later, John seemed like a modern-day Nostradamus.

In order for Zohran to win, Tarleton argued that three things were essential: a "youth quake" in voter turnout, a vast mobilization of South Asian and Muslim communities,[98] and a strong show of support from rent-stabilized tenants. While the city's matching funds gave Mamdani sufficient resources, Zohran's DSA-led field operation provided a

---

98 As the *New York Times* reported after the primary, there are approximately one million Muslims currently living in New York City.

volunteer army. As Tarleton forecasted, endorsements by AOC and the Working Families Party would help, and the two televised debates in June would give Zohran a chance to shine.

One major twist that no one could predict at the time was how Israel-Palestine would play out. *Politico*'s dubious Holocaust attack on Zohran, which went live the morning after the prescient *Indy* story came out, triggered a chain reaction. Although they were not enemies at the time, Brad Lander and Mamdani became much closer allies over the next month, bonding against the Israel hawks' weaponization of antisemitism in order to stoke Islamophobia.

On Friday, June 13, Zohran and Brad announced that they would cross-endorse each other. They did so in a lighthearted video shot in Central Park, with each candidate holding a Greek NYC coffee cup. On the night before the primary, the duo sat for an extended, not very scintillating interview on *Late Night with Stephen Colbert*.[99]

In the month after Tarleton's roadmap came out, Zohran received particularly helpful endorsements from ex-Rep. Jamaal Bowman, Public Advocate Jumaane Williams, the Working Families Party, AOC, and then the latter's mentor, Rep. Nydia Velázquez, who touted Mamdani's readiness to fight ICE deportations. As the early voting returns started rolling in on Saturday, June 14, things immediately looked good for Zohran. The large numbers of first-time

---

99 The host made Israel the primary focus of the discussion, leading *Defector*'s Samer Khalaf to observe that "Colbert grilled [Mamdani] harder than he did Donald Rumsfeld."

voters strongly suggested that those under thirty, along with many new South Asian and Muslim participants in the political process, were indeed casting ballots.

Harlem and Washington Heights, which have very sizable numbers of rent-stabilized tenants, produced extremely strong margins for Zohran, who benefited from hip-hop media influencer support. During the homestretch, Kid Mero cut a clip showing that younger folks uptown were very excited to meet the candidate they already knew so much about.

Progressive Black state senator Robert Jackson, a native son of Harlem, endorsed Zohran on June 18, with the pair walking the streets and riding the subway together. "Brought my brother-in-the-struggle uptown," the energetic 70-something Jackson told his Instagram followers.

An early endorsement from State Senator Gustavo Rivera (b. 1975) helped put Zohran on the map in the former's district that straddles Fordham Road in the central Bronx. Amid early voting, Michael Blake (b. 1982) and Mamdani cross-endorsed a few neighborhoods south of Rivera's, producing a quick video on Blake's home turf. As the former Bronx assemblyman later told me, after he and Cuomo's leading opponent cut the video, they walked around Morrisania. "The positive energy on the street was palpable," Blake said. "Zohran's momentum was real." Even though Cuomo captured more votes in the area, Mamdani still racked up numbers.

Mamdani scored big returns in Bed-Stuy, which, like Harlem, is experiencing rapid gentrification but still retains significant numbers of Black voters. Zohran's totals in both neighborhoods undermines the frequent claim made by the DSA's critics that only newcomers support socialist candidates. Overall, Cuomo still carried the city's mostly Black areas by sixteen points over Mamdani, but Mario's son had anticipated that his former base would produce much larger margins.

As housing activist Charlie Dulik detailed in *New York Focus*, renters came out in force for Zohran. In the city's 52 assembly districts in which tenants are the majority, Zohran defeated Cuomo by 12 points. Cuomo, by contrast, won 11 of the 13 homeowner-led districts. Of the 2.4 million city residents who live in rent-stabilized units, over 40% are immigrants, and roughly 75% are people of color.

"Many older Black voters in Crown Heights are rent stabilized and Zohran's rent freeze message really resonated with them," explained Phara Souffrant Forrest, the DSA assemblymember representing the district. Here, again, Cuomo's name recognition and longstanding ties to local leaders enabled him to win the area, but Zohran still gained ground.

Cuomo's inability to grasp why tenants embraced Zohran was on full display when he chatted with Errol Louis in mid-July, as the failed primary candidate started his general election campaign. As they walked around Cuomo's childhood neighborhood of Holliswood, Queens, an area with lots of large single-family houses, the NY1 host teed up a softball question about the importance of homeownership. The failed primary candidate struck out.

Homeowners, Cuomo told Louis, share a "culture of vest[ment] to their community." The longtime suburbanite contrasted those he viewed as neighborhood pillars to renters who come and go. He advised Louis that tenants, like hotel guests, are most concerned about "how many towels they use." In a studio interview with Errol a few nights later, Zohran called out Cuomo for denigrating the millions of city residents who do not own their homes.

*

During the hectic last week of the primary, Zohran carved out time to speak with Geo News, a Pakistan-based outlet. Speaking mostly in Urdu, liberal nightly TV host Shahzeb Khanzada asked Mamdani about how Jewish voters in New York City viewed what Khanzada called the genocide in Gaza. Answering mainly in English, the surging mayoral candidate explained that he was gaining increasing support from Jewish voters angry about Israel's war crimes.

Pakistani American voters in the city came out in force for Zohran. Brooklyn's "Little Pakistan," which runs along Coney Island Avenue in and around Kensington, produced plenty of Mamdani votes. After the victory, Gyro King, an area Pakistani restaurant, enticed the candidate's fans to a celebration in Prospect Park by offering over 500 free meals.

During the last few weeks of the race, Palestinian American leaders including Ruwa Romman, Georgia's pioneering Muslim elected official who was not allowed to take the stage at the 2024 Democratic National Convention, knocked on doors in Bay Ridge, Astoria, and the Bronx for Zohran. Across the five boroughs, neighborhoods with substantial numbers of South Asian and/or Muslim residents produced very strong returns for Mamdani.

Just before primary day, Egyptian American comedian Kareem Rahma's multi-platform series "SubwayTakes"—which has many Muslim fans—featured Zohran. The two pals discussed the socialist's agenda while using their MetroCards as faux microphones. Instagram influencer Wear the Peace helped the episode go viral.

As Democratic consultant Amit Singh Bagga documented on X, by the end of June 24, Yemenis in the East Bronx joined Bangladeshis in Kensington and a wide range of South Asians in Jackson Heights and central Queens in support of a candidate who looked like them. In many such areas, Zohran's first-round tallies more than doubled Eric Adams' totals from four years earlier.

Documented NY reported that Jagpreet Singh and DRUM Beats had "deployed volunteers speaking Urdu, Bengali, Punjabi, Nepali, Tibetan, and Guyanese Creole to conduct door-to-door outreach in immigrant neighborhoods across the city." Bagga's analysis showed that the efforts paid off. "When you talk to people in the languages that they speak, literally and proverbially, about issues that they care about, they respond," Amit stated. "And when you don't, they don't."

On the Saturday before the primary, NY Communities for Change (NYCC) joined the NYC-DSA, CAAAV, and DRUM for a spirited rally in Jackson Heights. As young speakers wearing hijabs denounced Trump's immigration crackdown, veteran Black and brown NYCC organizers held a banner bashing billionaires, while CAAAV activists hoisted a "Freeze the Rent" poster featuring a red dragon. Zohran showed up, tapped rhythmically on a tassa drum, then raced off to more campaign stops.

The following day, more than 100 volunteers came out to canvas for Zohran and Alexa Avilés in Sunset Park. On this Sunday afternoon, the surging mayoral candidate and the vicious antagonist who shouted about "antisemitism" were elsewhere. Jewish Voice for Peace, along with CAAAV and UAW Local 9A, brought out many members, with the DSA's trained canvass leaders furnishing instructions to door-knocking teams.

Mamdani volunteer John Whitlow, a CUNY Law professor, told me he saw "no organic expressions of support" for Cuomo while speaking to Sunset Park voters that afternoon. In the Chinatown section of the Brooklyn neighborhood, Zohran signs appeared in the windows of coffee shops frequented by younger East Asians. Unlike adjacent Boro Park, a Trump stronghold that overwhelmingly supported Cuomo, Sunset Park solidly backed the democratic socialist.

At the pre-canvas rally, Avilés showcased many of the hit mailers that Ackman, Loeb, and fellow Israel hawks had funded against her, with the councilwoman laughing at the absurd smears. DSA assemblymember Marcela Mitaynes (who joined Zohran's Friday night Manhattan march), told me that she and Alexa were confident that Avilés would win the primary, but now wanted to "run up the score."

Run Zohran Run!

Like progressive Shahana Hanif in the neighboring district, Avilés indeed crushed the Israel hawks' candidate.

In late July, the Board of Elections released full details regarding the ranked-choice voting process. After round one, Zohran 470,000 votes outnumbered Cuomo by over 80,000. Due mainly to the fact 75% of Lander supporters ranked him second, Mamdani's final tally surpassed the former frontrunner by 130,000. As the DSA's Aaron Narraph explained on X, in terms of total ballot mentions (or 1-5 rankings), Cuomo finished a distant fourth, trailing Mamdani, Lander, and Adrienne Adams. Along Sutton Place, the socialist even collected a few hundred votes.

Zohran's primary win is "one of the greatest accomplishments by the left and the socialist movement in the last century," NYC-DSA co-chair Gustavo Gordillo told *The Dig*'s Daniel Denvir during a two-hour-long podcast interview about the campaign. "We built a working-class coalition that expanded the electorate in a way that no one thought was possible anymore." While the socialists and fellow travelers did so without much support from organized labor, most of the city's leading unions quickly got on-board for Mamdani's general election run.

In late July, Amit Singh Bagga's research firm announced the findings of a recent extensive survey that showed Zohran receiving very strong support from nearly every demographic, from Asian voters to men of color, reform Jews to LGBTQ+ voters, and from women of color to public transportation riders.

Put differently, the historical record shows that during the 2025 primary, Zohran and company opened up two cans of whoop-ass.

*

"He's a 100% Communist Lunatic (CL)," Trump posted the day after the primary on Truth Social, the president's in-house platform. One week later, the petty tyrant declared that the CL "will destroy New York," questioned Zohran's citizenship status, and threatened to arrest Mamdani if he blocked ICE deportations. Trump's VP then blasted the socialist for not showing sufficient "gratitude" on the Fourth of July.[100]

In mid-July, the MAGA figurehead praised Cuomo, thus deflating the hopes Zohran's other main challengers, Mayor Eric Adams and Republican candidate Curtis Sliwa, who vied for DJT's blessing. In sync with Cuomo, White House Press Secretary Karoline Leavitt told reporters that the president "does not want to see *Zem-donny* elected."

Leading New York Democrats including Gov. Kathy Hochul (b. 1958) and Rep. Hakeem Jeffries (b. 1970) sharply criticized Trump's threats against Zohran, but as of the end of July, both party figureheads declined to endorse a mayoral candidate overwhelmingly selected by the Democrats' own voters. Sen. Chuck Schumer also withheld his support. So did Sen. Kirsten Gillibrand (b. 1966),

---

100 On July 4, Zohran tweeted: "America is beautiful, contradictory, unfinished. I am proud of our country, even as we constantly strive to make it better."

who slandered Mamdani by falsely telling WNYC's Brian Lehrer that Zohran had made "references to global jihad."

Gillibrand was forced to apologize. But she and the other top New York Dems faced minimal mainstream media pressure to support the party's candidate. While Zohran sought to make his cost-of-living agenda a centerpiece of the Democrats' national platform, the Schumer-led brass looked the other way.

Starting in the early 2000s, Schumer (b. 1950) has helped his party focus on issues faced by the middle class, and the Dems' loss of working-class support does not seem troubling to him. What really irks him is any criticism of a certain U.S. ally. "My job," as the senate minority leader recently explained to the *Times* right-wing columnist Bret Stephens, "is to keep the left pro-Israel."

Coming from someone who usually says nothing insightful, that is a very revealing statement. Given the direction of the left on Israel in recent years, Chuck clearly has not performed his self-assigned "job" successfully. But it is not hard to see why he disdains Zohran, whose pro-Palestine statements at rallies at Grand Army Plaza may still ring in the senior senator's ears.

Why Jeffries did not quickly follow the lead of Rep. Jerrold Nadler (b. 1947), the Upper West Side-based chair of the Congressional Jewish Caucus who immediately endorsed Mamdani after the primary, was not fully clear. The Democrats' top figure in the House cited his grave concerns regarding the "globalize the intifada" issue. In addition to his outspoken disdain for socialism, Hakeem has long been an ardent Israel supporter.

Jeffries is not an ally of Eric Adams,[101] so Cuomo appeared to be his only other option. Meanwhile, the results of the primary posed a problem for the aspiring House majority leader. Zohran won Hakeem's district by twelve points—and Jabari Brisport, the local DSA state senator, is waiting in the wings.

When she first ran for governor in 2022, Hochul assured the city's billionaire crowd that she would not support any effort by the state legislature to raise income taxes. Bipartisan deference to the 1% is a signature feature of the second Gilded Age. Hardly a minute passes in the national conversation without mention of a robber baron's name. As left-wing journalist Ken Klippenstein noted on X, CNN transitioned from a post-primary conversation with Zohran—during which the candidate stated that he "doesn't like capitalism"—to fluffy coverage of Jeff Bezos' $50 million wedding in Venice.

"I don't think we should have billionaires," Zohran told *Meet the Press* host Kristen Welker a few days after the primary, creating a stir. Faiz Shakir, Bernie Sanders' Pakistani American senior adviser, told an MSNBC panel that Mamdani should adopt FDR's notorious response to hostility from his foes among the economic elite. "Welcome their hatred," Shakir counseled.

As the Baby Boomer-Gen X ultra-rich count their money, tomorrow's leaders seek a more egalitarian future. A

---

101 In the 2021 primary, Jeffries backed Maya Wiley, marking one of the few times that he aligned with AOC in local races.

Run Zohran Run!

recent You.Gov survey found that 62% of US residents between the ages 18-29 view socialism favorably. In mid-July, *Drop Site*'s X account showed a clip of a podcast in which Andrew Schulz, a popular comedian, observed that Zohran's democratic socialist agenda is "what the base wants—what the people are into." "Honestly, that's what America wants," replied Charlamagne.

Many other stars circled Zohran's orbit in June. Comedians including pro-Palestine Saagar Shaikh and Asif Ali (stars of the *Deli Boys*) and Astoria-based lefty Stavros Halkias (*Tires*) joined West Village resident and pop icon Lorde in plugging the socialist.[102] On primary day, filmmaker Ava DuVernay chatted with Zohran on Instagram. That morning, supermodel Emily Ratajkowski, a longtime Bernie supporter, lit up the same platform by posting a clip in which she interacts with the socialist while sporting a Hot Girls for Zohran T-shirt. The fashionista group lent cheeky support throughout the campaign, most notably by hosting a Mamdani lookalike contest in mid-June.[103]

It is easy for both naysayers and hardcore activists to dismiss celebrity backing as mere attention-seeking by people who love to be in the public eye. But the Old Left's "cultural front" of the 1930s reeled in artistic support from Langston Hughes, Paul Robeson, Woody Guthrie,

---

102 Bill de Blasio's November 2013 victory party at Brooklyn's Bell House featured New Zealand-raised Lorde's "Royals," a neo-Leveller anthem.

103 *Saturday Night Live* stars Bowen Yang and Sarah Sherman also plugged Zohran, with Sherman posting a much-viewed TikTok chat with the candidate.

Dorothea Lange, and countless other legends. Three decades later, New Left and Black freedom struggle sentiments reverberated throughout rock and roll, Motown, and funk. The revolution requires hard work, but it can and should encourage creative expressions of every kind. Note to self: insert Kid Rock joke here.

How Zohran would handle the New York city's frightened, hyper-sensitive billionaires became an immediate concern because attention must be paid to this neglected lot. At a mid-July summit with the 1%, the socialist candidate reportedly did not recognize James Tisch, a right-wing entertainment mogul and leading figure in Israel support networks who sat in the first row. The high rollers wanted to know if Mamdani would retain Jim's daughter Jessica Tisch, a dour technocrat currently serving as Eric Adams' fourth NYPD commissioner in the former cop's current four-year term. Zohran reserved his decision.

On the first Saturday night after the primary, the triumphant candidate thanked his many supporters across the city. At the Barclays Center in Brooklyn, Zohran assured a roaring Haitian crowd that "we will stand up for Haiti because you taught the world about freedom." Across town at the Beacon Theatre, comedian Ramy Youssef invited Mamdani to the stage with the recently freed Mahmoud Khalil, thrilling the packed house. As Muslim poet Hanif Abdurraqib wrote in the *New Yorker*, "It was a delight to catch a glimpse of [Mahmoud and Zohran] laughing."[104]

---

104 Both Zohran and Mahmoud met with Bernie Sanders during separate July visits to DC, with Sanders posting smiling pics of himself with his arm around each figure.

Run Zohran Run!

Mamdani and his next-generation voters share a fundamentally different set of values from New York City's power elite. They are pro-Palestine and unafraid to be painted red. In describing Zohran's bases of support, voter turnout guru Michael Lange (b. 1999), an adviser to the campaign, coined the term "Commie Corridor" to describe the East River waterfront neighborhoods from Astoria south through Williamsburg that put up large numbers for the socialist. While many older voters view "commie" as a term of derision, twenty-somethings laugh at it.

*

"We are approaching the dawn of a new era in New York City," Zohran told reporters at a 5:30 a.m. presser in Astoria. Thus began a long day's journey into a night that saw the candidate hop about town before delivering his victory speech in Long Island City, then exchange hugs on the street with AOC.

After Cuomo's concession, the election-night celebrants chanted "A-li! A-li!" when Zohran's consigliere appeared on the big screen, in an interview broadcast live on NY1. The X feed of the Muslim Democratic Club, a group Najmi cofounded with Palestinian activist Linda Sarsour and others in 2015, called Ali "Zohran's brother and forever the People's Champ."

The next morning, Queens activist Jaslin Kaur posted a photo of herself with a middle-aged South Asian male fellow party attendee, with both showing their pearly white teeth to the camera while Lina Khan mingled in the background. "Last night," Kaur happily reported, "i stood next to the same taxi drivers and union members i went on hunger strike with as we watched our friend declare victory for mayor."

Kaur's lower-case "i" illustrates that no individual, including the candidate himself, can claim credit for Zohran's victory. But it was mostly certainly a triumph for the city's growing South Asian and/or Muslim communities, the DSA and kindred left-wing activists, Palestine supporters, hip-hop legions, and youth across the five boroughs. It was a resounding defeat for Mike Bloomberg and his friends at the *New York Times*, the *New York Post*, Bill Ackman, and Mario's son.

And let's not forget Whitney Tilson. Or perhaps we should.

"We all love this city, and yet it doesn't mean much if we can't afford to stay here," Zohran told the *Guardian*'s Erum Salam back in October. When the dust finally started to settle a few weeks after the primary, Donald Borenstein, Zohran for NYC's videographer, reflected on the campaign's efforts. The "most essential ingredient to our video style," Donald posted, was "a genuine love for the city and all of its people." Amid the torrent of hate he faced in the last six weeks of the campaign, Zohran frequently invoked his advocacy for "the city we love," often in sync with the June sunshine.

As we open the book on the politics of the future, let's close this chronicle with a blast from the past. At the *Hell Gate-New York Focus* mayoral forum at the Public Theater in mid-May, Zohran said that his favorite film about New York City is Spike Lee's *Do the Right Thing*, which

Run Zohran Run!

premiered during the racially charged 1989 Democratic primary contest pitting David Dinkins versus incumbent Ed Koch.

In a standout monologue, the film's pivotal character Radio Raheem (Bill Nunn) tells Mookie (Spike Lee) why he's wearing two sets of gold brass knuckles, with his right hand reading love and his left spelling out hate. "One hand is always fighting the other," Raheem says while shadowboxing on a Bed-Stuy block.

In the imaginary fight Raheem presents to the camera, hate first puts love "on the ropes," but love then makes a dramatic comeback, knocking out hate with repeated right-hand blows. "I love you," Raheem tells Mookie. The plot then spirals in the opposite direction.

Unlike in Lee's 1989 classic work, in New York City's 2025 Democratic primary, love triumphed.

—August 3, 2025
Sunset Park, Brooklyn

Note to readers: If you'd like to share anecdotes about your interactions with Zohran's campaign for possible inclusion in the post-general election edition of this book, please email RZR@ORBooks.com for guidelines.

Theodore Hamm is the author of *Bernie's Brooklyn: How Growing Up in the New Deal City Shaped Bernie Sanders' Politics*. He wrote about the 2025 race for The Indypendent and Drop Site, and his articles about New York City politics have also appeared in *Jacobin*. Hamm is chair of journalism at St. Joseph's University, NY in Clinton Hill, Brooklyn.